THE EMERGING CHURCH

—

IN EPHESIANS

THE EMERGING CHURCH

—

IN EPHESIANS

A. JOHN CARR

Foreword by Canon Roland Walls

CHARIS PUBLICATIONS
DUNDEE, SCOTLAND
Telephone (0382) 26372

Printed in Scotland, U.K., for
CHARIS PUBLICATIONS
58 Constitution Street,
DUNDEE. DD3 6NE.

by

CONTACT PRINTERS,
Albert Street, DUNDEE.

DEDICATION

First, to my Lord and Saviour, whose grace and love both captivated me, and by which I have been constrained to write and publish this book. Next, to my dear wife Jean, who through our twenty eight precious years of marriage has been unfaltering in her love, loyalty and devotion and without whom, this book could not have been written.

CONTENTS

FOREWORD   1

PREFACE   3

PREVIEW   7

PART 1
THE UNVEILING OF GOD'S PURPOSE IN THE CHURCH

1   THE CHURCH'S HERITAGE   13

2   THE HEADSHIP OF CHRIST   33

3   SO GREAT A SALVATION   45

4   THE UNITY OF THE SPIRIT   57

5   STEWARDS OF THE REVELATION   73

6   RESOURCES OF POWER AND LOVE   89

PART 2
THE OUTWORKING OF GOD'S PURPOSE THROUGH THE CHURCH

7   THE VISION FOR UNITY   103

8   WALKING IN THE LIGHT   127

9   THE SPIRIT'S FULNESS   143

10 MARRIAGE IN THE LORD   159

11 HOME AND BUSINESS   173

12 CONFLICT AND TRIUMPH   185

    POEM - 'THE VISION GLORIOUS'   201

ACKNOWLEDGMENTS

I am most grateful to Canon Roland Walls for his constant support and reassurance and for writing the Foreword. Amongst others who have had a part in this work and to whom I express my warmest appreciation are Miss C.McLarty who typed some of the earlies notes, Miss D.Gniady who spent several weeks revising and correcting the text, Miss F.Mulvie who patiently typed and prepared the whole work for the printer, and my son Stuart who designed the cover and offered some useful suggestions.

FOREWORD

One trustworthy sign of the new outpouring of the Holy Spirit upon the people of God is an awakened desire to read, mark, learn, and inwardly digest the Holy Scriptures; for here above all the Spirit fulfils the promise of Jesus that "He will not speak of Himself but He will take the things of mine and will show them unto you"

Today all over the world and across all our traditions and divisions there are emerging groups of Christians who sustain themselves with study and prayer round the Bible, as they feed from the table of the Word of God. Like the Ethiopian eunuch we need a Philip who will sit beside us and open up the Scriptures. Such a Philip is Pastor John Carr, whose friendship I count among the many gifts God has given me.

Here is a book from his pen which will take you into the very heart of the mysteries of God's love if it is read in the spirit in which it has been written. Through the words and thoughts of St. Paul you will begin to experience the reality of which the apostle speaks.

Here the letter to the Ephesians is restored to its rightful place as the inspired unveiling to the believer of "All the spiritual blessings of heaven in Christ (Eph.1:3), of how infinitely rich He is in grace (Eph.1:7), and of how we are to live the good life as He meant us to live it (Eph.2:10)". Here is an inexhaustible manual of Christian faith and life.

Have you as an individual or your Church as a congregation settled down in the rut of non-advancement? This is the book that will set you on your way again with a horizon of infinite possibilities as we make our own what we inherit in Christ.

It is unusual to find in the same author not only a burning enthusiasm but also such an ordered clarity of mind, that unerringly sets out the pattern of Paul's thought step by step. This is one of those books that we never just read and set aside - it is a book to *live with, to live out, to live by.*

There are many who, after the first experience of the Spirit's work in them, thirst for "wisdom and perception in what is revealed, who wish to see what hope God's call holds for us". (Eph.1:17,18). For them, this book will help towards maturity in Christ.

It is to be hoped that Brother John Carr will be moved by the Lord to pursue his studies in St. Paul's Letters and to add, one after another, expositions similar to this. Certainly, if you read his words you will have some idea of the depth of his understanding of the mystery of Christ.

May God bless the reader with the blessing Paul prayed for his original readers "That they might see how infinitely great is the power God has exercised for us believers". (Eph.2:19).

ROLAND WALLS.

Having meditated much in this epistle for over thirty years, I have become increasingly aware of its relevance in the rapidly and dramatically changing scene of this present era in the Church's life and history. The constraint upon me to teach and publish my present understanding, however limited, of the vision for our time, in this most revealing letter from the apostle Paul, has been quite overwhelming.

This book is based on a series of twelve lectures given to the second year students of the recently established Woodlands Bible College in Glasgow. I have not referred much to other authors or fathers in the faith who over the years have taught me so much of this truth, nor have I issued a bibliography of their important writings on this epistle. I am most grateful however, to any whose thoughts may be conveyed in these pages, and would like to mention in particular the invaluable help received from Dr.A.L. Greenway and the late Pastor W.L.Rowlands while studying at College.

My primary purpose for this publication is to help meet a pressing need in the Christian community arising out of totally differing concepts of what the Holy Spirit is doing in the lives of believers. Since the beginning of this century, the Holy Spirit has been moving in mighty waves of revival from time to time in many lands. Now, in all branches of the Christian Church there is emerging a large body of people who are submitting to and experiencing what is sometimes called 'Charismatic Renewal'. On the other hand there are many who do not understand this seeming phenomenon. Some of them, either through fear, or tradition, or even the pure motive of "contending earnestly for the faith", shrink from or even oppose what is happening. Sincere believers in both camps need enlightenment and direction. Those of us who humbly believe that we have received any measure of this, however inadequate it may seem to be, are held responsible for communicating it: "For unto whom-

soever much is given, of him shall be much required".
(Luke 12:48).

Since I personally happen to have been involved
in things 'pentecostal' or 'charismatic' from the early
days of youth, I have always sought to promote teaching concerning the ongoing, active work and ministry
of the Holy Spirit. Some believers who disapprove of
this, when faced with living and genuine examples
of practical experience in the Holy Spirit, claim that
these are too subjective and therefore dangerous. Thus,
while I still cannot imagine believers entering into
'new birth', 'transformed living', 'renewing of the
mind', 'forgiveness', 'broken heart', 'contrite spirit',
etc., without some degree of subjective experience,
it is essential that those in the 'charismatic camp'
observe this criticism and remember that subjective
experience must be related to objective truth. Without
this safeguard there is always the danger of imbalance.

In this book therefore, I have endeavoured to convey the essence of what I believe the Holy Spirit has
imparted to me. This I have done for the sake of sincere seekers on both sides. I have sought to write
simply, so that what the Holy Spirit is doing in all
branches of the Church will be related more to a sound
scriptural approach rather than any particular brand
or system of Theology.

For almost twenty years I have prayed and sought
earnestly to have any restricting theological or denominational mould in which I may have been cast,
broken: so that I may approach the Word of God
without prejudice or bias. This is not to despise the
past in any way, but, while rejecting irrelevant
trappings and traditions, and still holding fast to
that which is good, opportunity is thus created which
allows for a fresh understanding of what the Holy
Spirit is both saying and doing. In this connection,
literary or academic merit is not a prime concern.

If time is taken, prayerfully to study and meditate
on this epistle, one may feel, as I have felt, the very
pulsations of the apostle's heart-beat. For, concerning
this ministry, he declared: "I was made a minister,
according to the gift of the Grace of God....".

It is my prayer that not only will individuals
derive benefit from reading this book, but that groups
of believers will be helped in some way as they give

4

time to the study of this most illuminating of the apostle Paul's epistles.

In the College lecture notes, considerable reference was made to the original text, which was largely taken from the United Bible Societies' second edition of 'The Greek New Testament'. I also found the 'Analytical Greek Lexicon' published by Samuel Bagster and Sons most helpful. Students and others interested, may apply for these notes to the address inside the cover.

If this book makes any positive contribution to Christian believers' understanding of the vision of the unity of the Church, which is the Body of Christ, and the stewardship of its members, I will have good reason for thanksgiving to God Who caused His Grace to abound toward us.

A.John Carr.

Dundee,
SCOTLAND.

17 September, 1980.

What an enthralling, captivating epistle is this. I stand in awe at the revelation of truth it contains of the will and purpose of God in and through the Church, the Body, of Christ.

It is not enough to have received, or to be receiving a "Charismatic" experience. Thank God that "All over the world the Spirit is moving". But why? What is charismatic renewal for? The answer to this is as important as enjoying the experience itself.

The Holy Spirit is being poured out in these latter days to bring the Church on earth into that glorious unity for which Jesus Himself prayed - "That they all may be one; as Thou, Father, art in Me, and I in Thee, that they also may be one in us: that **THE WORLD** may believe that Thou hast sent Me". (John 17:21).

Jesus taught in John 1:16 that **THE WORLD** could not receive the Spirit of God but that the believers would. He also declared that when He, the Comforter, is come (to the believers), He would convict **THE WORLD** of sin, of righteousness and of judgment.

Paul received such a revelation of the purpose of God in and through the Church in the end time, that he declared that he was "as one born out of due time". (1 Cor.15:8). What he saw in vision for the Body of Christ would be for others following to enter into its fulfilment. This is God's time for His Church.

Of all that the apostle Paul was inspired to write concerning the Church, nothing is so comprehensive as that expounded in this epistle. It is to this that we have set ourselves the task of spending much time. To have the Holy Spirit impart revelation and inspiration to us, such as came to the apostle Paul, shall find us with him on our knees in wonder, awe and worship, as well as in the total commitment of our lives to Him, "who worketh all things after the counsel of His own will".

This epistle divides naturally into two principal

parts. First of all, chapters 1-3 contain **THE UNVEILING OF GOD'S PURPOSE IN THE CHURCH.** In this part we see -

1. _THE CHURCH'S HERITAGE_ (1:1-14)

Until believers come to understand what they are called to be, what they have inherited and what their position in Christ really is, they will continue by their own careless living, to denigrate and demean the grace of God before **THE WORLD.** We are no longer 'worms of the dust'. We are, through grace, 'Sons of God'. Everything about us now should be to the praise of the **GLORY OF HIS GRACE.**

2. _THE HEADSHIP OF CHRIST_ (1:15-23)

The Holy Spirit comes to bring wisdom and revelation to our own spirit, thus enlightening the eyes of our heart to enable us to grasp "what is the hope of His calling, and what the riches of the glory of His inheritance in the saints, and what is the exceeding greatness of His power to us-ward who believe". This introduces us to the overwhelming glory of Christ's Headship. He is not only Head over the Church, but "Head over all things" - principalities and powers, etc. - **"TO THE CHURCH".** His Headship, with its authority and total dominion, He has vested **IN THE CHURCH.** The Church is "His Body the fulness of Him ...." Hallelujah.

3. _SO GREAT A SALVATION (2:1-10)_

Here we are introduced to the all-embracing meaning of Salvation by grace. We are released from domination by satan to dominion in Christ, from death to life. We are quickened with Christ, raised with Him and seated in the heavenlies in Christ. The Church is now a colony of Heaven on earth. In eternity, the Church will display "the exceeding riches of **HIS GRACE".**

4. _THE UNITY OF THE SPIRIT_ (2:11-22)

The people of Israel had been especially privileged in having been chosen by God and thus had received the Law, the Covenants and promises etc. To and

through this nation would come the promised Messiah.
To all these privileges other ethnic races were
strangers and foreigners. "But now in Christ Jesus"
those who were "far off are made nigh by the Blood
of Christ". Through Christ, both Jew and Gentile "have
access by one Spirit unto the Father". There is now
neither need nor room for factions.

5. STEWARDS OF THE REVELATION (3:1-13)

Concerning this glorious revelation of the one
Church, the Body of Christ, the apostle Paul declared
that he had received a dispensation of the grace of
God. To him was committed the stewardship of this
ministry. To him, who was "less than the least of
all saints", had been given the grace to unfold to
all nations what had formerly been an undisclosed
mystery - the Church. The object of his ministry was
to make **ALL MEN** see their **STEWARDSHIP** of this
revelation.

6. RESOURCES OF POWER AND LOVE (3:14-21)

Apart from God's bounteous provision this may well
have been a beautiful ideal - yet unattainable.
But God has given to us His Spirit to impart dynamic
inward strength, producing within all members of the
Body the very life and nature of Jesus. Together
they experience the fulness of His love. What was
impossible to them before, is now gloriously possible
according to the power that works within them. Thus
is the glory of God manifest in the Church by Christ
Jesus now and evermore.

As we move into chapter 4, we are introduced to
the second part: **THE OUTWORKING OF GOD'S PURPOSE
THROUGH THE CHURCH.**

7. THE VISION FOR UNITY (4:1-16)

No longer can the members do their own isolated
or segregated thing. In the light of the vision
unfolded and the resources available, all can walk
worthily of their calling - keeping the unity of the
Spirit, growing up into Christ, the Head, and being
fully joined and functioning together.

9

8. WALKING IN THE LIGHT *(4:17-5:13)*

Since the Church is a colony of Heaven on earth no longer does it walk in the darkness of this world system. All the members walk as children of light. *"Arise, shine, for thy light is come .... His glory shall be seen upon thee"*.

9. THE SPIRIT'S FULNESS *(5:14-21)*

The Church lives constantly by the ongoing infilling of the Holy Spirit. By this all its behaviour is affected; its dedication and its life of worship and fellowship. The relationship of all its members is a delight as they submit one to another in the fear of God.

10. MARRIAGE IN THE LORD *(5:22-33)*

In Christian marriage, both husband and wife are fulfilled in each other and in their divinely ordained roles joyously live in the realm of submission and love. The glory of this is that such a marriage reflects the mystery of the relationship between Christ and His Church.

11. HOME AND BUSINESS *(6:1-9)*

This life of the Spirit manifests itself in the rightness of relationships in the family between parents and children, and in business between servants and masters. Right there the Church lives in the power of the Spirit.

12. CONFLICT AND TRIUMPH *(6:10-24)*

Thus finally, in and through the Church now seated in the heavenlies, our reigning Lord - the Head of the Church - is manifestly seen to have prevailed. Did He not say - *"I will build **My Church**; and the gates of hell shall not prevail against it"*?

1. Paul, an apostle of Jesus Christ by the will of God, to the saints which are at Ephesus, and to the faithful in Christ Jesus:

2. Grace be to you, and peace, from God our Father, and from the Lord Jesus Christ.

3. Blessed be the God and Father of our Lord Jesus Christ, who hath blessed us with all spiritual blessings in heavenly places in Christ:

4. According as he hath chosen us in him before the foundation of the world, that we should be holy and without blame before him in love:

5. Having predestinated us unto the adoption of children by Jesus Christ to himself, according to the good pleasure of his will.

6. To the praise of the glory of his grace, wherein he hath made us accepted in the beloved.

7. In whom we have redemption through his blood, the forgiveness of sins, according to the riches of his grace;

8. Wherein he hath abounded toward us in all wisdom and prudence;

9. Having made known unto us the mystery of his will, according to his good pleasure which he hath purposed in himself:

10. That in the dispensation of the fulness of times he might gather together in one all things in Christ, both which are in heaven, and which are on earth; even in him:

11. In whom also we have obtained an inheritance, being predestinated according to the purpose of him who worketh all things after the counsel of his own will:

12. That we should be to the praise of his glory, who first trusted in Christ.

13. In whom ye also trusted, after that ye heard the word of truth, the gospel of your salvation: in whom also after that ye believed, ye were sealed with that holy Spirit of promise.

14. Which is the earnest of our inheritance until the redemption of the purchased possession, unto the praise of his glory.

PART 1

THE UNVEILING OF GOD'S PURPOSE IN THE CHURCH

CHAPTER 1

THE CHURCH'S HERITAGE

(Ephesians 1:1-14)

1.	Grace in the Fellowship of Saints	(1:1,2)
2.	Grace in Life and Worship	(1:3)
3.	Grace in Divine Election	(1:4)
4.	Grace in Predestination	(1:5,6)
5.	Grace in Redemption	(1:7)
6.	Grace in Revelation	(1:8-10)
7.	Grace in the Inheritance of Saints	(1:11-13)
8.	Grace in the Sealing by the Spirit	(1:13-14)

CHAPTER 1

THE CHURCH'S HERITAGE

1   GRACE IN THE FELLOWSHIP OF SAINTS   (1:1,2)

"Paul, an apostle of Jesus Christ ...." This phrase
expresses conviction, confidence and authority. There
is no dubiety or double-mindedness here. Paul is sure
of his call. He has been commissioned as an
apostle - a sent one of Jesus Christ.

In reasserting the gospel he was proclaiming, he
made reference to those who had seen the Lord in the
post-resurrection era - *"After that, he was seen of
James: then of all the apostles. And last of all he
was seen of me also, as of one born out of due time.
For I am the least of the apostles, that am not meet
to be called an apostle, because I persecuted the
church of God. But by the grace of God I am what
I am: ...."* (1 Cor.15:7-10).

It has been suggested, that a necessary qual-
ification for an apostolic calling was, that one
should have seen the Lord face to face, and that
Paul could claim apostleship on this account. Simply
seeing the Lord, however, did not in itself make Paul
an apostle. It was his spectacular conversion that
brought him to acknowledge and to submit to Christ's
Lordship. Only then did he become aware of God's
elective purpose in his life. To Ananias the Lord said,
*"Go thy way: for he is a chosen vessel unto me, to
bear my name before the Gentiles, and kings, and
the children of Israel: for I will shew him how great
things he must suffer for my name's sake".*
(Acts 9:15,16).

He is bold to declare to the Galatians - *"Paul,
an apostle, (not of men, neither by man, but by
Jesus Christ, and God the Father, who raised him from
the dead:)".* (Gal.1:1). *"He that wrought effectually
in Peter to the apostleship of the circumcision, the
same was mighty in me toward the Gentiles: And when*

14

James, Cephas, and John, ... perceived the grace that was given unto me, they gave to me and Barnabas the right hands of fellowship; that we should go unto the heathen, and they unto the circumcision". (Gal.2:8,9).

He is assured and convinced of his calling and setting in the purpose of God and is fearless in declaring this. Before King Agrippa he is unequivocal. (Acts 26:13-19).

His personal statement in 1 Cor.15:8 that he was "born out of due time" is quite revealing. The words basically refer to an abortion - or that which is prematurely born - "before the due time".

He is indeed conscious of the fact that he was called to be an apostle, not just for the Church's earlier, more formative years - but for the Church's later and final years of completion and consummation. He saw the Church as the one Body of Christ, established, mature, complete. His vision and ministry were something that extended far beyond the limited confines of the era of his own earthly pilgrimage and extends right down to our time, when there are constant signs of the Spirit of God moving to reveal the Church in unity and glory - the living expression of the fulness of Christ. Here was an apostle with vision and revelation for our time.

"By (by means of) the will of God". Recognition and acceptance of his calling in life was really vital to the apostle Paul. It should be thus with all of us - every believer. Outside of this there is nothing but despair and frustration.

Paul's apostolic calling was not of his own choosing and deciding. God has an **eternal purpose** in Christ Jesus and since it is all in Him it involves us, His Church: for the Church is one with Him, is in Him, the very fulness of Him who fills all in all. Since it is only the purpose of God that matters and will finally prevail, and the will of God at any given time can conform only to and harmonise with its glorious outworking, then we had better get to know "what the will of the Lord is". This is much in Paul's mind:

The good pleasure of His will	1:5
The mystery of His will	1:9
The counsel of His will	1:11
The understanding of His will	5:17

This understanding of the will of God is available to every believer, but is not received by those who go their own way, do their own thing, walk in the flesh, or for any reason at all, live in some measure estranged from Him who has called them.

The fact, that there is a divine purpose and that God's will shall be accomplished, does not in any way imply that there is room for neglect, indifference or apathy on the part of the believer. Indeed, the very opposite is the case. The recognition, understanding, and acceptance of the will of God carries with it responsibility to everyone involved so much so that the apostle Peter makes a strong appeal right at the commencement of his second letter: "**Give diligence** to make your calling and election sure". (2 Peter 1:10).

The apostle Paul is positive, sure and clear. In the centre of God's will he has His peace, the anointing of His Spirit and all his ministry bears the marks of Divine inspiration. Thus, confidence and conviction are transmitted to all whose hearts are prepared to receive the Word. To be able to minister thus with authority and conviction is vital. We cannot be at peace, nor can we function as we should, unless we are convinced of the will of God for our lives and walk in it.

"To the saints .... and faithful in Christ Jesus". The ministry penned in this letter is sent out to specific people - to the saints and faithful in Christ Jesus. Here is ministry for and to the Church, and applicable only to those who are part of it. Such people are clearly described and thus positively identified. They are saints, i.e. **holy ones** and they are faithful in Christ Jesus. They bear the marks of the new creation, of the work of divine grace upon them and within them - of the renewing of the Holy Ghost. They are characterised also by a sense of responsibility, by faithfulness in Christ Jesus.

Those who are faithful in Christ Jesus are those who are fully conscious of their calling. Their response to God is constant and consistent. Faithfulness is the hallmark of their lives and of their conduct and communion.This letter is unmeaningful and inapplicable to those who are not found amongst the Holy Ones and faithful in Christ Jesus. Let us settle it in our hearts, before we take a step further into this sacred territory, that we truly are those to whom this letter is written.

"Grace be to you, and peace, from God our Father, and from the Lord Jesus Christ". While this is a fairly normal salutation of the apostle Paul, it is much more. His earnest desire is that God's people be characterised by **GRACE** and **PEACE**. Nothing of what God has wrought in His full and finished work in Christ could possibly be on any other basis. "And the Word was made flesh, and dwelt among us, (and we beheld His glory, the glory as of the only begotten of the Father,) full of grace and truth .... And of His fulness have all we received, and grace for grace". (John 1:14,16).

The advent of Christ was a revelation of divine grace in its fulness. In our receiving of Him there has been poured into us of His fulness - Grace upon Grace. So, when the apostle Paul describes his own calling, he says - "He called me by His grace". (Gal.1:15). "I am the least ...., not meet to be called an apostle ...., But by the grace of God I am what I am: .... I laboured .... yet not I, but the **GRACE** of God which was with me". (1 Cor.15:9,10). "I was made a minister, according to the gift of the grace of God given unto me .... Unto me, who am less than the least of all saints, is this grace given ...." (Eph.3:7,8).

By the 'grace of God' we mean .... divine favour, undeserved, unmerited, unearned - freely bestowed. Not only is one accepted by it, but one is also filled with it and his whole life expresses it.

It is in this beautiful sense that the apostle Paul portrays his earnest desire for God's people - "Grace be to you ...." Everything he is and has is wholly of grace, and all that he is and does henceforth must be expressive of it. The fulness of grace poured in is poured out to the blessing of all.

Once we have seen and accept that everything we are, have and do are wholly of His grace and that the only glory that will engender praise is the "glory of His grace" - then the inevitable result is that of **peace**. The struggle and strain are over - we enter into rest. It is the experience of divine grace in one's life that produces **PEACE** of heart and mind.

We have learned over the years the value of this

peace of which Jesus said: "Peace I leave with you, my peace I give unto you: .... Let not your heart be troubled, neither let it be afraid". (John 14:27). This too was the very first ministry of the Risen Christ on Resurrection day to the assembled, distraught disciples: - "Peace be unto you". (John 20:19). If ever there was a practical demonstration of grace and peace it was on this occasion. Here was peace .... "By the blood of Christ ...." (Eph.2:13,14). This is peace that:

(1) Reconciles to God. (Rom.5:1)
(2) Reconciles us to one another. (Eph.2:14,17,18)
(3) Garrisons heart and mind. (Phil.4:7)

The grace of God in Christ was revealed for this very purpose - "For He is our peace ...." Only those who have fully received the grace of God know His peace. The lack of this peace clearly indicates the existence of something that is outwith the ministry of His grace, e.g. self-will, self-desire, carnal thinking, carnal effort — "For to be carnally minded is death; but to be spiritually minded is life and peace". (Rom.8:6). In all His communion with men, God can only operate in the realm of His grace. Thus, both the grace and the peace are from God our Father and from the Lord Jesus Christ.

This 'grace and peace' principle is at the very heart of fellowship amongst believers. Where God's grace is wholly at work, unhindered by carnality, self, disobedience etc., the fruit of that is PEACE. It is thus on the ground of grace and peace that all God's work is wrought, or else it would be characterised by confusion, restlessness and all the characteristics of the flesh. "For God is not the author of confusion, but of peace, as in all churches of the saints". (1 Cor.14:33). James has some enlightenment for us on this subject in his epistle. (James 3:11-18).

2 GRACE IN LIFE AND WORSHIP (1:3)

"Blessed be the God and Father of our Lord Jesus Christ". Kenneth Wuest translates these words thus: "May the God and Father of our Lord Jesus Christ be eulogised". A eulogy is a speech or writing in commendation or praise. To eulogise, therefore, is to extol or praise.

In Paul's experience, God no longer is a remote, unknowable being beyond one's reach, but One who has, in the person of His only begotten Son, drawn near and identified Himself with man, and to him has become a living, relevant reality. The God, whom Paul now worships, is the Father of our Lord Jesus Christ, and since all that is divine, all that is of grace and truth, and all the light of the knowledge of the glory of God he now sees manifested in the person of Jesus Christ alone - God has become so real, that his prime objective now is to worship Him. All his revelation of God is seen now in the person of His Son, and God has become meaningful, understandable, approachable, relevant. The Christ, whom he had formerly rejected and bitterly opposed, has become the centre and circumference of all his life and purpose. The whole purpose of God for man, and for time and for the fulness of times and for eternity, he sees in Christ alone. He can only worship Him.

"Blessed be ...." Here is worship that is expressed in language. It is worship that is communicated. Everything about us then, whether it be the language of the life or the language of the lips, commends the Lord: speaks well of Him. He is worthy of praise and blessing. In the light of the revelation of Himself in Christ and of His eternal purpose in Christ, which involves and includes us, we cannot but stand in awe before Him. We simply bow in humble and loving reverence, spontaneously ejaculating, both in our own tongue and the new tongue, the wonderful praises of the Lord.

"Who hath blessed us with all spiritual blessings in the heavenlies in Christ". All three words here, related to "blessing", have the same root meaning. The idea of "speaking well" is basic to them all. So it is not only we, who in our worship speak words of praise and blessing to God - but God's blessing to His saints has to do with God speaking well - God speaking commendably to and of us.

One thing is absolutely clear - all of God's blessing upon His people is bound up with "His Word" and is never divorced from it.

God spoke His word to Abraham, and said, "By myself have I sworn, saith the Lord, for because thou hast done this thing, and hast not withheld thy son, thine only son. That in blessing I will bless thee ....; And in thy seed shall all the nations of the earth be blessed; because thou hast obeyed my voice". (Gen.22:16-18). The writer to the Hebrews said - "When God **made promise** to Abraham, because He could swear by no greater, He sware by Himself, saying, Surely blessing I will bless thee ...." (Heb.6:13-14). And Paul to the Galatians says - "So then they which be of faith are blessed with faithful Abraham". (Gal.3:9).

Over and over, the idea of blessing relates vitally to the spoken word, and the fulfilling of that blessing relates to our believing, accepting and obeying that word. So divine blessing in the believer's life has to do with the Word of God and the faith, that comes both from the hearing and understanding of the Word and then holds fast to it. "Abraham believed God, and it was counted unto him for righteousness".

By this time, the apostle Paul has been given such a revelation of Christ whereby he knows that all, absolutely all, of divine blessing to the saints is in Christ alone. It is not something to which we may look forward, or that God has promised to enact in the indeterminate future, but that which has been wholly wrought, completed, finished in Christ. He **has** blessed us. Sadly, not all believers see it this way. Far too many are still waiting for God to do for them what He has already done.

God has spoken - it is finished. Christ is not only the author, but the finisher of our faith. He is indeed "Alpha and Omega, the beginning and the ending". "God, who at sundry times and in divers manners spake in time past .... by the prophets, hath in these last days spoken unto us **by His Son**". (Heb.1:1,2). He is the Word, which God has spoken, who "was made flesh, and dwelt among us" - (Logos). He has become the very Word of faith that we preach - (Rhēma).

Of all creation, God made only man in His own image. In man alone is the ability to communicate thought by language - by the spoken word. Through-out the history of mankind God has made His mind clearly known by His spoken word. How precious it is that when we hear, accept, believe and obey God, we then become aware of divine blessing. By faith we enter into every blessing that God has spoken and revealed.

The apostle James recognised the power of the spoken word, as did the old patriarchs, the early apostles and our Lord Himself. "What a word is this", they spoke of Him, - "for with authority and power He commandeth the unclean spirits, and they come out". "For He taught them as one having authority, and not as the scribes".

The account given in Genesis 27:27-30 of Isaac blessing his son Jacob instead of Esau, is exceedingly touching and revealing. Neither of these men had any doubt whatsoever about the effectiveness of the blessing imparted, though it was conveyed but by spoken words. "Isaac blessed him (Jacob) and SAID, ... And it came to pass, as soon as Isaac had made an end of blessing Jacob ...."

Clearly this blessing was imparted by words. There was no doubt in Jacob or Esau's mind concerning the weight and authority of these words. When Esau discovered how Jacob had supplanted him, both in the matter of the birthright and of the father's blessing, he cried out - "Hast thou but one blessing, my father? bless me, even me also, O my father. And Esau lifted up his voice, and wept". (Gen.27:38).

The father's blessing was sought for, received and unquestioningly believed. For when Esau discovered that the blessing, which he should have claimed, had been spoken to Jacob instead, he never thought for one moment of trying to reverse it. One wicked thought entered his mind - "And Esau hated Jacob because of the blessing wherewith his father blessed him:and Esau said in his heart. The days of mourning for my father are at hand; then will I slay my brother Jacob". (Gen.27:41).

The tragedy of many professing believers in these days is that they spend so much time seeking divine blessing that there is so little evidence of real blessing. One is forced to wonder why? Is it not because God has spoken, but

(1) We have not heard what has been said.
(2) We try to read into it what we think is said.

(3) For these and other reasons faith has not laid hold on the Word.

(4) We sometimes hear intellectually but not spiritually.

(5) We sometimes wait for God to do what He has already done.

Let us remember that He has blessed us with every spiritual blessing in Christ. It is done. Why then do so relatively few appropriate the blessings already provided?

These blessings are called "spiritual blessings". They are revealed, communicated, grasped by the work of the Holy Spirit. All the blessings in Christ Jesus become a reality to us only by the Spirit of God. It is only the Holy Spirit who can take of the things of Christ and convey them to our understanding - "Eye hath not seen, nor ear heard, neither have entered into the heart of man, the things which God hath prepared for them that love Him. But God hath revealed them unto us by His Spirit .... that we might know the things that are freely given to us of God". (1 Cor.2:9-12).

That is why the apostle Paul also tells the Corinthians - "God also hath made us able ministers of the New Testament; not of the letter, but of the Spirit: for the letter killeth, but the Spirit giveth life". (2 Cor.3:6). Only the Spirit of God can make clear what God has said; only by Him can faith arise in our hearts - for faith cometh by hearing, and understanding of the Word of God; but even then it is not acquired by intellectual attainment - in our spirit we know what is of the Spirit of God and this is what enlightens our intellect, not our academics, however desirable and necessary these may be.

All this blessing - is "In Christ". Here then is the wonder and measure of God's grace: actually "accepted in the Beloved". Literally everything about this great salvation is "In Christ". This is not all, however: these blessings are "In the heavenlies in Christ". To understand and appropriate this is to introduce the Body of Christ to the fullest dimension available to every believer.

The rest of the epistle clearly unfolds the meaning

of this most enlightening phrase:

(1) *"Blessed us with all spiritual blessings in Christ".*
   THIS IS THE CHURCH'S SPHERE OF LIFE (1:3)

(2) *"Set Him at His own right hand in the heavenlies".*
   BECAUSE THIS IS WHERE CHRIST IS   (1:20)

(3) *"Made us sit together in the heavenlies in Christ Jesus"*
   AND SHE IS SEATED THERE WITH HIM   (2:6)

(4) *"Now unto the principalities and powers in the heavenlies might be known by the Church the manifold wisdom of God"*
   THUS IT IS THERE SHE DISPLAYS GOD'S MANIFOLD WISDOM   (3:10)

(5) *"We wrestle .... against spiritual wickedness in the heavenlies".*
   THUS TO OVERCOME IN THIS VERY SPHERE   (6:12)

   IN CHRIST ALONE - BY THE SPIRIT

3 GRACE IN DIVINE ELECTION (1:4)

"According as He hath chosen us in Him before the foundation of the world, that we should be holy and without blame before Him in love".

The words "He hath chosen us" literally mean "He picked us out". This is one of the blessings spoken of in verse 3. The doctrine of 'Divine Election' has been the cause of endless debate in theological circles and sometimes the focal point of some of the most bitter controversies.

These controversies largely rage around the subject of 'Free Will' and 'Predestination'. If we formulate a system of theology with undue emphasis on one of these themes to the exclusion of the other, we become unbalanced. These two major issues have been analogously described as a pair of railway lines running together, side by side throughout the scriptures. To remove one of the rails is to court disaster.

There are a few considerations to be taken into account, as we meditate on this great theme of 'Divine Election'.

i. 'Divine Election' reflects the sovereignty of God. No one dictates to God. Election secures to God that His will shall be accomplished.

ii. This was a predetermined sovereign act of God. God is not careless, haphazard or arbitrary in His plans. He knows what He is doing. He decrees in accordance with His own sovereign will. Before the laying down of the foundation of the cosmos, this whole world system, 'God chose'.

> *"Deep in unfathomable mines*
> *Of never-failing skill,*
> *He treasures up His bright designs,*
> *And works His sovereign will".*

(W.Cowper)

iii. The Election of God is "In Christ" alone. Only "In Him" could God purpose to have a people who would be conformed to His image. Thus from the very dawn of creation - in His inscrutable thought - Christ was already "The Lamb slain from the foundation of the world". (Rev.13:8).

iv. Since 'Divine Election' is "in Christ" alone, then it is all of grace. When we understand the grace of God, we will cease from our endeavours to limit God according to our own carnal thinking, even in this great subject of Election.

v. Once it has dawned upon believers that God has chosen them "in Christ", there comes an excitement, accompanied by humble thankfulness, that God had them in His thought. When God gave His Son, it was His chosen ones whom He had in mind.

vi. At this point, no endeavour should be made to theorise about people not being chosen. Whether the main issue of Election is either that of the people chosen or the purpose for being chosen, we are not to be wise above what is written. So we cease from speculative theories of either the inclusive or exclusive aspect of Election.

vii. The verb used is in the middle voice and simply means - "God chose us for Himself". Even at a human level it is good to feel wanted. What a thrill to know that God wanted us for Himself.

viii. Perhaps the most important aspect of 'Divine Election' is the purpose of it. Why did God choose? "That we should be holy and without blame before Him in love". This truth is overwhelming. Such is our position "In Christ" that we can now, not only in the future, stand before, or in the sight of a Holy God - holy and blameless. Such is the abounding nature of His grace.

4   GRACE IN PREDESTINATION   (1:5,6)

"Having predestinated us" - means *"Having ordained us beforehand"*. This pre-ordaining by God was for a specific purpose: *"Unto the adoption of children by Jesus Christ to Himself"*. The word 'adoption' - huiothesian - means 'To place in the condition of a son' - from huios meaning 'Son' and tithēmi meaning 'to set, with design, in a certain arrangement or position'. This is the word used in 1 Cor.12, *"God hath set the members .... "* (v.18) and *"God hath set some in the church"* (v.28).

Therefore, God has chosen and predestined the saints to be placed, by definite design, as sons in His own family. By this, believers are made *"heirs of God, and joint-heirs with Christ"*. (Rom.8:17). *"For both He that sanctifieth and they who are sanctified are all of one: for which cause He is not ashamed to call them brethren"*. (Heb.2:11).

"According to the good pleasure of His will". The outworking of and fulfilling of 'The will of God' is delightful and joyous, both to God and to us.

Romans 8:29 says *"For whom He did foreknow, He also did predestinate to be conformed to the image of His Son"*. Christian believers are uniquely distinct from all other people, since, *"In Christ"*, they are placed into God's family as His sons. The Sonship of Jesus Christ Himself is unique in that He is the **ONLY-BEGOTTEN** Son of God. Believers, on the other hand, are through grace, the 'Sons of God' by adoption.

"To the praise of the glory of His grace, wherein He hath made us accepted in the beloved". From the

context it is quite clear that this means - "For us to be to the praise ...." In Christ we are chosen so that we should be holy and without blame before Him. In love He has predestinated us to the adoption of sonship.

He is the "God of all grace". The apostle Paul has captured something of the glory of that grace as he beholds the church "In Christ". Everything about the church of God should be a revelation of the glory of God's grace. This is the glory that is seen in Jesus Christ - "We beheld His glory .... as of the only begotten of the Father, full of grace and truth. (John 1:14). The object of all praise should be the glory of the grace of God as revealed in Jesus Christ our Saviour and Lord. The Greek word for "Accepted" is used only twice in the New Testament, both in this text and in Luke 1:28 - "Hail, thou that art highly favoured". It means 'much graced'.

Just as Mary was 'highly favoured' - 'much graced' to become the sacred means for the bringing to birth of the Christ Child - so the Church is 'highly favoured' to be the vehicle for bringing forth Christ in all His fulness. "The church, which is .... the fulness of Him ...." (Eph.1:23).

But it is all "In Christ". All the fulness of divine grace is "in Him" - only as we are found in "the beloved" can we ever reveal Christ Himself in all His fulness. Concerning Jesus Christ the Father could say "My beloved Son, in whom I am well pleased". (Matt.3:17). Everything about Jesus brings pleasure to His heart. Everything about us had been cause for grief, but such is the magnitude of the grace with which He has visited us, that He has "made us accepted in the beloved". Now He does not see us as we were, but as we are "in Christ". Thus, in Him, we too bring pleasure to the heart of God. All who are "in the beloved" are a cause for our heavenly Father's delight.

Later in the chapter, Paul talks about "The riches of the glory of His inheritance in the saints". It is time to cease belittling the wonder of His grace. No longer are we 'worms of the dust' - but 'sons of God': "If any man be in Christ, he is a new creature: old things are passed away; behold, all things *are become new" (2 Cor.5:17).*

5 GRACE IN REDEMPTION *(1:7)*

"In whom we have redemption through His blood, the forgiveness of sins, according to the riches of His grace".

The verb for 'To redeem' - *lutroō* - used e.g. in Titus 2:14, 1 Peter 1:18, means 'To release for ransom paid'. Here, however, the noun for redemption is 'apolutrōsis', and means 'To dismiss for ransom paid'. The ransom price of the blood of Christ has been paid. God's holy law has been satisfied. Not only has God's righteous law no more claim on us, but "in Christ" the law itself says 'I dismiss you, I want nothing more to do with you. The ransom price has been fully paid and adequate provision fully made by the abounding riches of God's grace'.

The law and sin have no more claim on us now and since the verb "We have" is continuous present tense, it means that **ALL THE TIME** we should be enjoying the total freedom from the law's demands and sin's dominating power. We should enjoy the freedom afforded us by the riches of His grace.

At the heart of this word 'Redemption' is the word -*luō*, meaning 'To set free'. There is total freedom, deliverance from sin.

In Romans 8:22,23 we read "That the whole creation groaneth and travaileth in pain together until now .... waiting for .... the redemption of our body". The redemption of the body is yet to be realised when mortality puts on immortality, and this corruption puts on incorruption. In the continuous present tense, we are enjoying redemption now: deliverance from sin; deliverance from our offences; deliverance from all bondage. The time is yet to come, however, when redemption will be seen to be deliverance from the very presence of sin. Then there will be freedom from the whole scene of sin. In verse 14 we read - "Which is the earnest of our inheritance until" - or for, or to - "the redemption of the purchased possession, unto the praise of His glory". Clearly, therefore, redemption in that sense is still to be fully realised.

We have redemption now, however. "We have" -
continuous present tense - "redemption through His
blood". That is the fountain of His grace - 'The blood
of Christ'. "If we walk in the light, as He' is in the
light, we have fellowship one with another", and His
blood goes on keeping us clean. (1 John 1:7).

6 GRACE IN REVELATION (1:8-10)

"Wherein He hath abounded toward us in all wisdom
and prudence; Having made known unto us the mystery
of His will".

First of all, let us notice that what abounds
towards us is "The riches of His grace". What has
been bestowed upon us in the abounding riches of His
grace are wisdom, prudence (right-mindedness or
intelligence) and revelation - "Having made known
unto us the mystery of His will".

The apostle Paul's calling was by revelation
(Gal.1:1) and the ministry, which he received and
communicated, was by revelation (Gal.1:11,12;
Eph.3:3). Until the Holy Spirit came at Pentecost, the
vision of the 'Church, which is His Body' was not
made known "unto the sons of men, as it is now
revealed unto His holy apostles and prophets by the
Spirit". (Eph.3:5).

The wisdom, intelligence and enlightened understanding are the work of the Spirit. The revelation
received was from above, given by the Spirit. Whenever
the word 'Mystery' is used in this epistle, it means
'A secret knowable only by revelation'. This is what
is now imparted to the church, says the apostle, but
the important thing is that all of this is only because
God made His grace abound toward us.

Consequently, in the church and in the ministry,
there is no room for fleshly pride, worldly wisdom,
or self-glory. The only glory is that of the grace of
God. Thus, He has "made known unto us the mystery
of His will, according to His good pleasure which He
hath purposed in Himself". In the dispensation, in
the plan (oikonomian), in the economy of God, in God's
scheme and administration for the fulness of times,
He will gather everything in heaven and earth
together under one headship, even "in Christ".

"All things in Christ, both which are in heaven,

and which are on earth; even in Him".

To this end, He is now preparing His church for a tremendous role and function in that final dispensation. That is why the Headship of Christ to the church is all-important, as is the principle of Headship manifest in the church amongst the members. Now the church is subject to Christ's Headship. Then all things in heaven and earth will be.

7 *GRACE IN THE INHERITANCE OF SAINTS* *(1:11-13)*

"In whom also we have obtained an inheritance ...." It is a sobering and humbling thought, that, in all God's eternal purpose and plan, through His grace He has included us. We have already mentioned that we are heirs of God and joint-heirs with Christ. In all the eternal purpose of God in Christ Jesus our Lord, we are privileged *"in Christ"* to have obtained an inheritance.

"That we should be to the praise of His glory, who first trusted in Christ. In whom ye also trusted, after that ye heard the word of truth" - or having heard the word of truth, - *"the gospel of your salvation: in whom also after that ye believed ...."* This is something done, an action already completed. People take the doctrines of grace and eternal security etc. and say we have absolutely nothing to do at all, that we do not even have to respond. But here we have the individual's response - *"After that ye heard the word of truth, the gospel of your salvation: .... ye believed"*. Paul is saying - 'We first trusted .... then you trusted, after having heard ....' Thank God for His grace revealed *"in Christ"* - and the grace and faith imparted, both inviting us and enabling us to respond.

8 *GRACE IN THE SEALING BY THE SPIRIT* *(1:13,14)*

"Ye were sealed with that holy Spirit of promise. Which is the earnest of our inheritance until the redemption of the purchased possession, unto the praise of His glory". 'To seal' means to 'mark distinctly as invested with a certain character'. We have the stamp of God upon us. We are invested not with a theology that presumes upon the grace of God,

but with a distinctive character which reveals the grace of God, which is characteristic of the divine nature. This is the new nature - Christ in us. That can be and shall be for ever. This sealing of God follows the act of our believing. When we confess our faith in the Lord Jesus Christ alone and wholly submit to His Lordship in our life, in every area, God by His Holy Spirit stamps us with the seal of His divine character. This is "the earnest" (the pledge, the foretaste) "of our inheritance until the redemption of the purchased possession" - until that day when it will be seen to be complete.

In Ephesians 4:10 we have the statement - "Whereby ye are sealed unto the day of redemption". It is exactly the same word in the aorist tense, meaning - 'Ye were sealed - ye were stamped with the seal of God, with the seal of His divine nature'. From chapter 4 of the epistle, we see the response and responsibility of the believers as they relate to every member in the Body of Christ. In the Body of Christ dwells "the fulness of Him that filleth all in all". But the response and responsibility of the believer is seen in his walk, and how he conducts his life.

God is sovereign. Through grace, He has done everything for us "in Christ", concerning our salvation and His eternal purpose. God has done it all "in Christ". This, however, does not relieve us of the responsibility of walking worthily. If God's seal is upon us, it will be revealed in our walk. One who walks in the light, the seal of God will mark out until the day of redemption.

When we see what God has for us and our position "in Christ"; when we walk as "sons of God" with the stamp of God upon us; when we relate together as God intends us to do in the whole Body of Christ: then the church will be the revelation of the living, exalted Christ of God. Then will people see that Christ is alive, feel His presence and power and bow the knee and acknowledge that Jesus Christ is Lord.

Ephesians 1:15-23

15. Wherefore I also, after I heard of your faith in the Lord Jesus, and love unto all the saints,
16. Cease not to give thanks for you, making mention of you in my prayers;
17. That the God of our Lord Jesus Christ, the Father of glory, may give unto you the spirit of wisdom and revelation in the knowledge of him:
18. The eyes of your understanding being enlightened; that ye may know what is the hope of his calling, and what the riches of the glory of his inheritance in the saints,
19. And what is the exceeding greatness of his power to us-ward who believe, according to the working of his mighty power,
20. Which he wrought in Christ, when he raised him from the dead, and set him at his own right hand in the heavenly places,
21. Far above all principality, and power, and might, and dominion, and every name that is named, not only in this world, but also in that which is to come:
22. And hath put all things under his feet, and gave him to be the head over all things to the church,
23. Which is his body, the fulness of him that filleth all in all.

CHAPTER 2

THE HEADSHIP OF CHRIST

(Ephesians 1:15-23)

1.   Fellowship under Christ's Headship   (1:15,16)

2.   Enlightenment under Christ's Headship   (1:17,18)

3.   Privileges under Christ's Headship   (1:18-20)

4.   Dominion of Christ's Headship   (1:21,22)

5.   Manifestation of Christ's Headship   (1:22,23)

CHAPTER 2

THE HEADSHIP OF CHRIST

1 *FELLOWSHIP UNDER CHRIST'S HEADSHIP* (1:15,16)

This portion of the Ephesian epistle deals essentially with the glorious theme of 'The Headship of Christ'. The apostle Paul understood clearly that the church would be built no matter what assailed it, either from within or without, because Christ Himself is "Head over all things to the church, which is His body".

The vision of "the church, which is His body" was just emerging as a completely new revelation, committed to the apostles and prophets by the Spirit. The apostle Paul considered himself strangely privileged in receiving this enlightenment. What was happening to believers in their lives and relationships was exciting. He could see that all this was not only possible, but was actually happening before his very eyes, confirming the dominion which Christ Himself now possessed and exercised in His Headship.

Paul had not been in Ephesus for some time. A few years had elapsed since he last met the elders of the Ephesian church at Miletus (Acts 20:17). News had come to him, while he was imprisoned in Rome, which caused him to state in his letter .... "After I heard of your faith in the Lord Jesus, and love unto all the saints, Cease not to give thanks for you ...." Although Paul himself was now unable to continue his ministry in the same way as before, under Christ's Headship the Church would go on. The apostle's heart rejoiced at the news received and he gave thanks to God.

The full revelation, of what was really happening in the outworking of divine purpose, had not yet gripped the believers. This, however, did not prevent them from enjoying the blessing of their new life in Christ.

The fellowship of the saints at Ephesus was

34

exemplary in its character. Two basic elements shone through it all. First, "Faith in the Lord Jesus" and secondly, "Love unto all the saints". When believers are firmly established in Christ, then fellowship with each other is no problem. Faith in the Lord Jesus is vital to "love unto all the saints". In this kind of life and fellowship 'Faith' reaches up to our Lord producing 'Love' within us that flows out to all around.

Without going into the meaning of faith here, we can be sure that "Faith in the Lord Jesus" means that we are rightly related to Him in terms of identification, commitment, submission, co-operation obedience, etc. That being the case, this vital relationship with Him will manifest itself in the outgoing life of one to the other. This too will be impartial - "Love unto **ALL** the saints".

This epistle does not encourage isolated Christian believers, who seek to fulfil their own individualistic conception of Christ and His truth. The emphasis is not on believers in their personal walk, but concerns the responsibility and relationship of members in the Body of Christ. The Lord Jesus Christ is not promoting individualism: He is concerned with His eternal purpose being manifested in "the Church, which is His Body." This whole epistle unveils the mystery of the Body of Christ.

Why we do not see the fulness of Christ manifested is not because we necessarily fail as individuals. Rather, it is because ofttimes we fail to understand that, as individuals, we are but part of the whole. It is the whole Body of Christ that expresses "the fulness of Him that filleth all in all". Everything about Christ, all His fulness, indwells His Body. The Church, His Body, is called to be the revelation of Himself.

Later, Paul describes this "love unto all the saints". This 'agapē' love surpasses knowledge, yet we can grasp with all the saints "what is the breadth, and length, and depth, and height" of it. Having become rooted and grounded in it, we go on to experience in fellowship the fulness of it. When our faith is right in the Lord Jesus, the outflow is of love to all the saints, irrespective of what denomination, tradition or branch of the Christian

Church to which they belong.

These are the basic elements of true fellowship in the Body of Christ. In such, the atmosphere breathes of divine blessing; the anointing of God's Holy Spirit is manifest; peace and joy abound; help, comfort and encouragement are present; and above all, the conditions are perfect for further illumination to the Body by the Holy Spirit.

2 ENLIGHTENMENT UNDER CHRIST'S HEADSHIP (1:17,18)

Paul's prayer was that "God .... may give unto you the spirit of wisdom and revelation in the knowledge of Him: The eyes of your understanding being enlightened".

It was not sufficient for the apostle Paul that the saints were enjoying their salvation and their fellowship. There is always the danger of settling down at a certain level in our Christian experience. Just simply to accept the blessings poured out and not to be enlightened about the ways and purpose of God, will keep God's people in the spiritual category of 'infants', never leaving the stage of immaturity.

"He made known His ways unto Moses, His acts unto the children of Israel". (Psalm 103:7). Some people are content to see what God is doing and share in the blessing of it. But to know God's ways and have understanding by revelation of the Holy Spirit: these belong to the mature and responsible ones.

What was at the heart of the apostle's prayer for the saints was that they come into the deeper knowledge of God Himself, so that there would be the opening of the eyes of their understanding: literally, 'The eyes of your heart' - i.e. the seat of one's mental frame or intellect and feeling. This is not the kind of understanding that dwells coldly in the realm of mere intellect, but that which relates to one's very heart. It is not enough to have an objective grasp, but one that subjectively and experientially grips our whole personality.

How does this kind of "knowledge of Him" come about? Paul prays that "the God of our Lord Jesus Christ, the Father of glory may give unto you the spirit of wisdom and revelation in the knowledge of Him. This means that God's moving by His Holy Spirit *is in the realm of one's spirit.*

In chapter three of this book we shall examine how believers have been 'quickened', or made alive in their spirit. We shall also be looking at the relationship between one's spirit and one's mind, noting particularly the distinction between spirit, soul and body - and how these inter-relate in one's personality.

Clearly, it is only as we 'come alive' in our spirit and the Holy Spirit brings wisdom and revelation, that our minds and hearts are illuminated with understanding.

There is only one "Spirit of wisdom and revelation" - that is, the Holy Spirit. He is "the Spirit of wisdom and revelation". He is the One Who reveals the things of God. In John's Gospel, Jesus gives us some very enlightening insights into the work and the ministry of the Holy Spirit.

To have wisdom and revelation one must have the Spirit of God operating within him. One must allow the Spirit of God to communicate to his spirit. He and the Spirit of God are one. In that way, one is led by the Spirit of God. He lives the fulness of life that is in Christ, and by grace shares His very life when, in a real sense, his own spirit becomes a "spirit of wisdom and revelation".

Because of the oneness relationship of the Holy Spirit with the believer's spirit - "He that is joined unto the Lord is one spirit" - his own spirit, as it is anointed and inspired by the Spirit of God, becomes itself a "spirit of wisdom and revelation". This is the very thing for which Paul prayed.

When we are in this spiritual way with God, then "The eyes of our understanding are enlightened". Our minds themselves are not the source of the things we come to know. Did our mind reason out that we are, or how we became, children of God? Our mind could never have grasped this understanding without our being enlightened by a "spirit of wisdom and revelation". Romans 12:2 speaks of the "renewing of your mind"; and Ephesians 4:23 - "Be renewed in the spirit of your mind", i.e. 'your spirit that controls, disciplines and enlightens your mind'. With this renewing, our minds cease being subject to the dictates of carnal and humanistic ideas, which are without foundation and confusing. Such enlightened, renewed and sound minds are minds that are disciplined by the Spirit of God, or by our spirits as they relate to the Holy Spirit. "For God hath not given us the spirit of fear; but of power, and of love, and of a sound mind". (2 Tim.1:7).

In 1 Thess.5:23 Paul says, "I pray God (will sanctify) your whole spirit and soul and body". He did not say body, soul and spirit, because the first thing in our lives is not our body, nor is it our soul with its soulish, sentimental, emotional fluctuations. First - the quickening of our spirit, then - our soul with its mental and emotional life renewed, disciplined, enlightened. "For as a man thinketh in his heart so is he". It is in the realm of his reasoning and understanding that he conducts his life. He lives according to the dictates of his mind. What he wills, reasons, purposes - that is what he is and that is what he does. Thus it is utterly essential to have a renewed mind, a disciplined mind - literally, an enlightened mind.

We have been looking at how we come to understand spiritual things, the things of God. We cannot know these things by mere academic attainment. They are not understood by carnal or fleshly wisdom. We can know spiritual things only by revelation: revelation imparted by the Holy Spirit to our spirit. He is thus referred to as "the Spirit of wisdom and revelation", for God desires to impart both. Wisdom and revelation are not the same. Revelation is God disclosing what had been a hidden mystery. The word 'mystery' in Ephesians means 'A secret knowable only by revelation'.

In 1 Cor.2:9-10 we read, "Eye hath not seen .... But God hath revealed them unto us by His Spirit ...." If God were, however, to impart only revelation and no wisdom by the Holy Spirit, thus illuminating our understanding, that would enable us to behold it and to know about it, but not necessarily to experience it. There are many believers like that whose eyes have been opened and who can see precious things by the Spirit of God, but they do not live in the good of them. They do not enter into the inheritance that is theirs in Christ.

Paul did not just pray that we might receive a spirit of revelation only, but a spirit of wisdom also. It is one thing to know, but quite another to appropriate what is known. We need wisdom for this as well as revelation. Hence this prayer of the apostle, that we may receive a "spirit of wisdom and revelation". It is not enough to receive light and revelation only. We need wisdom also, to enable us to apply ourselves to that which God has revealed for the whole of our life, so that both revelation and experience in our daily walk will go hand in hand.

So many people come to know God in an objective way. To really know God is not merely to have an intellectual assessment of Him. To know Him is to be one with Him; to be on speaking terms and in vital communion with Him. This is why we receive the "spirit of wisdom and revelation". It is to bring us into that close, spiritual and intimate knowledge of Him. In this sense God and we are one.

Only on this basis can we know all that is to follow in this epistle. Our new and eternal life in Christ springs out of this kind of knowledge. "This is life eternal, that they might know Thee the only true God ...." (John 17:3). This is the very essence of life that is divine, the spiritual life which, by the wisdom and revelation imparted, brings us into a communion with God where we know Him in very truth.

It does not matter how long we have been on the way, nor how much learning we have had, but rather how open our heart is to receive from God, so that by faith we appropriate what is of His Spirit. After many years some have never advanced much beyond the regeneration stage. Paul had to say to the Corinthians, "I .... could not speak unto you as unto spiritual, but as unto carnal, even as unto babes in Christ. I have fed you with milk, and not with meat: for hitherto ye were not able to bear it ...." (1 Cor.3:1,2). Thus it is only as His Spirit and our spirit become one (1 Cor.6:17), that we grow in grace and in the knowledge of our Lord Jesus Christ.

3 PRIVILEGES UNDER CHRIST'S HEADSHIP (1:18-20)

What is this enlightened understanding about? What

knowledge have we acquired with this enlightened understanding? Firstly - "what is the hope of His calling". Secondly - "what the riches of the glory of His inheritance in the saints". Thirdly - "what is the exceeding greatness" - the surpassing greatness - "of His power to us-ward who believe".

Notice where the emphasis lies.

> The hope of HIS (GOD'S) calling of the saints.
> The glory of HIS (GOD'S) inheritance in the saints.
> The greatness of HIS (GOD'S) power to the saints.

The manward concept of the Church puts the emphasis on 'our calling', 'our inheritance', 'our power'. The enlightenment brought to us by the Spirit of God, however, puts the emphasis Godward, where it truly belongs.

The very concept of the 'Church' - ecclēsia, from 'ek' meaning 'out of' and 'kaleō' meaning 'to call', is that of an assembly of God's people, 'called out' by God. It is a distinctive, unique people called out of worldliness, sin, self-motivation, etc.: a people delivered from the authority of darkness and translated into the kingdom of His dear Son. (Col.1:13).

Included in the "hope of His calling" are the following insights: "that now unto the principalities and powers in heavenly places **might be known by the church** the manifold wisdom of God. According to the eternal purpose which He purposed in Christ Jesus our Lord". (Eph.3:10,11). "That He might **present it to Himself a glorious church**, not having spot, or wrinkle, or any such thing; but that it should be holy and without blemish". (Eph.5:27). "That in the ages to come He **might shew the exceeding riches of His grace** in His kindness toward us through Christ Jesus". (Eph.2:7).

To know "what is the hope of His calling", in this way, liberates God's people from the childish, immature, fleshly attitudes and motives, that would keep them waging their warfare against flesh and blood. This is what gives meaning and purpose to the believer's life.

"The riches of the glory of His inheritance in the saints". It is good to identify with the apostle Peter, who reminds us that we are begotten "To an inheritance incorruptible, and undefiled, and that fadeth not away, reserved in heaven for you". (1 Peter 1:4): or even with the apostle Paul, who said that the Spirit's seal was "The earnest of our inheritance". (Eph.1:14). It is, however, even more elevating to have illumination concerning the "riches of the glory of His inheritance in the saints".

This revelation, of the magnitude and glory of God's grace in His saints, is most awesome and inspiring. Man - in creation since the Fall - is corrupt, vile, depraved and totally lost, but - in redemption the Church, His saints, display the riches of the glory of God's inheritance. The Church becomes the very habitation for God Himself by the Spirit. (Eph.2:22).

How important it is to receive this revelation by the Holy Spirit. It lifts believers from the 'Condemnation' complex, the 'worm of the dust' concept and restores again, through divine grace alone, the glory of being 'Sons of God' - 'Saints of God', thus becoming the vehicle for the manifestation of Christ in His fulness.

"And what is the exceeding greatness of His power to us-ward who believe". This is the same power which Jesus promised would be imparted to His disciples when the Holy Ghost would come upon them. (Acts 1:8).

When we see how relatively impotent and powerless (what we call) the Church seems to be, we realise how imperative it is that the eyes of our understanding be enlightened. May God deliver His people from the blindness that paralyses them through ignorance of the dynamic power of God, available to all believers by faith. It is little wonder that Paul prayed this prayer for the saints and faithful in Christ.

With the understanding of God's provision comes faith enabling us to appropriate it. Those who believe are those who have seen and understood, and within whom faith has risen up and been released by a total thankful acceptance and commitment. Their trust is in God alone, bringing them into active co-operation with Him and the obedience of faith.

This is why the apostle Paul prayed that the saints would be "strengthened with might" - (dunamis) - "in the inner man". (Eph.3:16). His confession of faith was that He is "able to do exceeding abundantly above all that we ask or think, according to the power that worketh in us". (Eph.3:20). His exhortation in the face of spiritual conflict was "be strong" - with power. "Be strong in the Lord, and in the power of His might". (Eph.6:10).

As we look at the next section, we will see clearly the character and magnitude of that power available and potentially resident in the Church of Jesus Christ.

4 DOMINION OF CHRIST'S HEADSHIP (1:21,22)

It is important to know the purpose which the apostle Paul had, in describing the nature and magnitude of the dominion of Christ in His Headship. All members of the Body of Christ should be alive to the fact that all powers, forces and authorities finally have to submit to Christ's ruling authority. "All power (authority) is given unto Me in heaven and in earth". (Matt.28:18). He reigns supreme.

He desired the whole Church to know that "the exceeding greatness of His power to us-ward who believe", is "according to the working of His mighty power".

First of all, this working of God's mighty power is demonstrated in Christ's resurrection - literally 'having raised Him from among the dead'.

Secondly, in His ascension 'And (Him) having seated at His right hand, in the heavenlies'. God in Christ, has demonstrated His might and ability, in His dominion over death, hell and the grave.

Thirdly, this continuing, unending, absolute reigning authority which Christ has, is described in v.21 and literally translates 'above and beyond every chief, and authority, and power, and Lordship, and every name that is named, not only in this age, but also in the settled future'.

Thus, there is no prince, authority, power or lordship, over which or whom Christ has not dominion - now, or evermore. That is the nature and extent of the power of God available to the Church.

5 MANIFESTATION OF CHRIST'S HEADSHIP (1:22,23)

"And hath put all things under his feet, and gave him to be Head over all things to the Church".

From Col.1:18 we know *"He is the Head of the Body, the Church".* In that epistle, however, it is also clear that *"He is the Head of all principality and power".* (Col.2:10). Every conceivable power and authority, now and in the settled future, are completely under the feet of Christ's pre-eminent reigning authority. He is Lord of all.

Christ is not only the **Head of the Church** - He is rather **"Head over all things TO THE CHURCH".** This means that "the Church, which is His Body," which is "the **FULNESS** of Him that filleth **ALL IN ALL**,"* has vested in it, Christ's reigning authority. It is in this awe-inspiring sense that the Church has within itself dominion over all authorities, placed under Christ's feet.

In fact, as was pointed out in the last chapter, the Church has been blessed with every spiritual blessing in Christ *"in the heavenlies"*, for that is where Christ is - seated in reigning authority and glory.

Thus, every blessing available to the Church is *"in Christ"*, who has completely borne sin's judgment and broken its power, dethroned the evil usurper, triumphed over death and removed its sting for every believer, who has ascended to the Throne of God - to the place of supreme authority - *"in the heavenlies"* - and who demonstrates in and through the Church, *(to which as Head He is joined)*, His manifold wisdom and power.

---

* "The Church .... the fulness of Him that filleth all in all". This is the usual (almost universal) translation of the verb 'pleroumenou' treating it as "middle" but it could be passive, then the thought would be "The Church .... the fulness of Him who all in all is being fulfilled" - a picture of the Christ progressively reaching His full extent and compass by incorporating us into His Body by the Spirit". (R.W.)

(See Armitage Robinson, 'Ephesians': Macmillan).

EPHESIANS 2:1-10

1. And you hath he quickened, who were dead in trespasses and sins;

2. Wherein in time past ye walked according to the course of this world, according to the prince of the power of the air, the spirit that now worketh in the children of disobedience:

3. Among whom also we all had our conversation in times past in the lusts of our flesh, fulfilling the desires of the flesh and of the mind; and were by nature the children of wrath, even as others.

4. But God, who is rich in mercy, for his great love wherewith he loved us,

5. Even when we were dead in sins, hath quickened us together with Christ, (by grace ye are saved;)

6. And hath raised us up together, and made us sit together in heavenly places in Christ Jesus:

7. That in the ages to come he might shew the exceeding riches of his grace in his kindness toward us through Christ Jesus.

8. For by grace are ye saved through faith; and that not of yourselves: it is the gift of God;

9. Not of works, lest any man should boast.

10. For we are his workmanship, created in Christ Jesus unto good works, which God hath before ordained that we should walk in them.

CHAPTER 3

SO GREAT A SALVATION

(Ephesians 2:1-10)

1. SALVATION - GOD'S REMEDY FOR HUMAN DEPRAVITY
   (2:1-3)

   Spiritual Death
   Satanic Domination
   Fleshly Living
   Soulish Living

2. SALVATION - GOD'S PROVISION FOR A REIGNING CHURCH
   (2:4-6)

   The Church Reigning in New Life
   The Church Reigning in Resurrection Life
   The Church Reigning in Ascension Life

3. SALVATION - GOD'S REVELATION OF DIVINE GRACE
   (2:7-10)

   Grace Displayed in Future Ages
   Grace Revealed in Imparted Faith
   Grace Demonstrated in Transformed Living

SO GREAT A SALVATION

1   SALVATION – GOD'S REMEDY FOR HUMAN DEPRAVITY

SPIRITUAL DEATH   (2:1-3)

"And you .... who were dead in trespasses and sins". Here we have what at first appears to be a paradox. Believers are referred to as being "dead", yet this is followed by a full description of the behaviour that had at the same time characterised their existence. How do we understand that people, who are "dead", can be spoken of as living? We may reply that they are spiritually "dead". What then do we mean by spiritual death?

It is necessary to learn, from the Word of God, how the human personality is constituted. We read in 1 Thess.5:23 – "I pray God your whole spirit and soul and body ...." Paul was speaking about the whole person, the whole man, the whole personality, and he described this personality as tripartite: spirit, soul and body.

The Greek word for spirit is *'pneuma'* – from which we get such words as pneumatic etc. and has to do with wind, breath, air. The word for soul is *'psuchē'* – from which we get psychology, psychic etc. – things relating to the mind. The word for body is *'sōma'*. In medical usage the word psychosomatic means bodily ailment or disease, either brought on or affected, in some way, by one's state of mind.

"Because man is 'spirit' he is capable of God-consciousness and of communion with God (Job 32:8; Psalm 18:28; Prov.20:27); because he is 'soul' he has self-consciousness (Psalm 13:2;42:5,6,11); because he is 'body' he has, through his senses, world-consciousness (Gen.1:26; Rom.7:23,24)". (Schofield Notes p.1270.)

In his state of spiritual death, therefore, man's

God-consciousness and hence his communion with God is basically extinct. The spirit, therefore, is that part of the personality that is not alive to God until quickened again, i.e. regenerated by the Spirit of God in the new birth. (John 3:7).

Since man's God-consciousness is marred by spiritual death, his conscience (a faculty of the spirit) is also affected. Conscience is that conscious-ness of a moral law that man has within him, intended for his moral and spiritual guidance.

Conscience, however, can only relate to the highest it knows. The loss of God-consciousness brings a dullness to the conscience which often insensitively interprets moral law according to degenerate human standards, leaving itself wide open to all kinds of satanic and evil influences. That is why, in salvation, man's very conscience is, by the blood of Christ, purged "from dead works to serve the living God". (Heb.9:14).

The soul is the self-conscious part of us, so that has to do with mind, reason, will, emotions and affections. By it one becomes conscious of self, of personality.

The body has physical senses through which the human personality relates to the environment around it. Through the physical senses, one's organs and members, every part of one's physical being - one's body - is in touch with and conscious of the surrounding world.

Thus we read in the text - "And you .... who were dead" - or existing in a state of death. That is the way the original text puts it. So one is existing - but not as a whole person. That is the unregenerate state. In this existence one cannot know true whole-ness or a sense of fulfilment. There is an aching void in one's life, something tragically amiss or desperately lacking. In this state, life is not just what it is meant to be. Thus, those who are unregenerate exist in a state of death.

SATANIC DOMINATION

"Dead", it goes on to say, "in trespasses and sins; Wherein in time past" - or formerly - "ye walked" - you lived your manner of life - "according to the course of this world". The Greek word for course is 'aiōna' - and the word for world is 'kosmos'. This means - 'according to the life, or state of things marking an age or era, the present order of nature'. You lived according to the state of things that distinctly mark the present order of nature.

Here we are introduced to the true nature of things in society. Man lost his God-given dominion when he submitted to the dominating, deceiving influence of satan. In man's obstinate, rebellious, anti-God state, satanic forces are constantly at work fostering unrighteousness, atheism, materialism, occultism, alcoholism, drug addiction etc.

The whole world system outside of the grace of God is in this bondage. The grace of God permits it only until God's appointed time, when He, who is "Head over all things to the Church", will be seen, as is prophetically stated in Psalm 110, to make His foes His footstool. It is this spirit that pervades the very atmosphere under the chief of the authority of the air. Satan is "the prince of the power of the air, the spirit that now worketh in the children of disobedience" - or obstinacy.

FLESHLY LIVING

"Among whom" - or in whom - "also we all had our conversation" - or conducted ourselves - "in times past," or formerly - "in the lusts of our flesh". 'Sarkos' is the word for flesh and does not simply mean body, which is only matter. It is the body as related to the soul. While we are thinking of spirit, soul and body separately in considering the human personality, it is important to see this tripartite being as a single human entity. "And the Lord God formed man of the **dust** of the ground, and breathed into his nostrils the **breath** of life; and man became a **living soul**". (Gen.2:7).

One cannot always be clear about the division between soul and body - where one ends and the other begins. They are vitally inter-related. One cannot say where is the seat of his emotions, or his affections. It is more than in the head or in the thinking. It affects one's whole personality. It affects one's body, inner, mental, and other aspects of one's *life pertaining to the senses.*

Therefore, when the Word of God speaks of "fulfilling the desires of the flesh", it refers to the effect of the sinful soul on the lusting body and vice versa. In this way, we have the prostitution of what should normally be legitimate physical desires.

One's body has natural appetites for things, that are in themselves quite proper. Even in one's relationships there are legitimate desires, that God has put in the human body, which cry out for fulfilment, but because man exists in a state of death, there is an imbalance in his personality. The spirit, or God-consciousness is missing and there is an estrangement from God. Thus the propensities, desires, lusts and the will of body and soul without God are what is meant by the lusts of the flesh. This is the human nature without God, the carnal nature.

And of the mind - "Fulfilling the desires of the flesh and of the mind". The word mind is in the plural - dianoiōn - the soulish part, and means 'the thoughts and the modes of feeling'. It is not just one lusting act. Some people go on living like this - in fleshly conduct. When men are spiritually dead, lacking God-consciousness and become dominated by sin, the very sensitivity of the feelings and desires of the soul are gone, till a man lives in the realm of his physical lusts and cannot, by himself, extricate himself from them.

SOULISH LIVING.

There are believers who sometimes mistake life on the soulish level for life in the realm of the spirit. If God-consciousness depended only upon feelings, desires, thoughts, yearnings, emotions and affections - our concept of and communion with God would vary according to the resulting state of mind. That is how some people tend to be. Their lives are up and down. They conduct their lives on the soulish level.

Believers are not intended to live their lives according to the feelings or sensations in the body. In themselves they are perfectly natural and God-given, but exceedingly subject to extreme variation. Neither are believers meant to depend on the emotions

and affections of the soul - for these too are subject
to constant change. E.g. Human love operates in the
realm of the soul and everyone knows of the nature
and limitation of this.

The soul, therefore, was never designed to be the
sphere of God-consciousness or of divine communion.
It is too temperamental and subject to too many unholy
influences. The soul may well express spiritual life,
but is never the source of it. The quickened spirit
fulfils this role, "But he that is joined unto the Lord
is one spirit". (1 Cor.6:17).

2 SALVATION - GOD'S PROVISION FOR A REIGNING CHURCH

(2:4-6)

Notice that from verse 3 there is a change in the
personal pronouns from second to first person. 'You
.... who were dead', 'Ye walked'. Then 'also we all
had our conversation'. 'He loved us'. 'We were dead'.
'He quickened us together'.

Although the apostle Paul defines and contrasts
in this chapter between 'YOU Gentiles' and 'US Jews'
and emphasises the differences in background and
tradition, he clearly points out that we were all
equally affected by the depravity of human nature.

"But God, who is rich in mercy, for his great love
wherewith he loved us," has in His marvellous grace
brought salvation to us all. "By grace ye are saved".

THE CHURCH REIGNING IN NEW LIFE

"Even when we were dead in sins, hath quickened
us together with Christ". The word 'quickened' -
sunedzōopoiēsen - should be noted primarily for two
reasons. It is, first of all, a compound word
constructed from three main roots - sun - 'together
with', dzoē - 'life' and poieō - 'to make', hence it
really means 'made alive together with'. Secondly,
it is in the aorist tense, meaning that it is already
an accomplished fact - completed in the past.

Thus, the apostle Paul is showing forth that God's
great salvation is not something designed merely to
meet our desperate need as isolated individuals, but
that He had the whole Church in mind. All of us
together were quickened with Christ.

This 'coming to new life' is not something to expect in the uncertain future, but takes us right back to the tomb, where Jesus was laid after His crucifixion. It was in that tomb that He came alive. This concept of our 'coming alive' together with Christ defies understanding by carnal thinking, or explanation by human logic and reasoning: but it is gloriously real to faith.

THE CHURCH REIGNING IN RESURRECTION LIFE

"And hath raised us up together". The word raised is again a compound word meaning - to raise together with, which means that the whole Church has been 'raised up together' with Christ. It is also in the same tense as the word for 'quickened' and reveals that it is already an accomplished fact.

Some people have a very limited concept of salvation - for them it does not go beyond the 'coming to life' stage. It seems that they come alive, but keep their grave clothes on and stay in the tomb. The faith God has imparted, to all who are willing to receive, moves into the realm of the resurrection life of our Lord. We are 'raised up together' with Him.

We remember, from chapter 1 of the epistle that His resurrection was 'out from among the dead'. May God open our eyes to see that this is already accomplished and all we have to do is to begin to live in the good of His resurrection life and fulness.

THE CHURCH REIGNING IN ASCENSION LIFE

"And made us sit together in the heavenlies in Christ Jesus". The construction of the word - 'to seat together with' is exactly the same as the two former words. It is already an accomplished fact that, in the ascension of our Lord, when He was set at His Father's own right hand in the heavenlies - the whole Church was included. No logic can explain this any more than it can explain the meaning of Charles Wesley's hymn - "He breaks the power of cancelled sin". But to all who believe, it is a glorious reality.

This is where the Church of Christ belongs - "In the heavenlies" - where Christ is. Thus, since He is set 'far above' all other powers and authorities - and all things are "under His feet", then with and in Christ the Church is in a reigning position and should not be subject to oppressive, dominating forces of evil that seek to intrude.

Remember that the "prince of the power of the air" operates amongst "the children of disobedience", but for all who have submitted to Christ the Lord and repented of their rebellion, they are quickened, raised and seated together with Christ. While some of the Church are already at home with the Lord, the remaining visible part of the Church dwells on earth, but by faith and "in Christ" we are already seated "in the heavenlies". That means that we are a colony of heaven on earth.

If we had known only resurrection life, we would still be subjected to the dominating power of the forces of evil, but since we enjoy ascension life, we literally "reign in life by one, Jesus Christ". (Rom.5:17).

3   SALVATION - GOD'S REVELATION OF DIVINE GRACE

GRACE DISPLAYED IN FUTURE AGES   (2:7-10)

"That in the ages to come he might shew the exceeding riches of his grace ...." "By grace are ye saved". Salvation by the grace of God must not be seen as simply that initial new birth experience - that 'quickening' with new life. The salvation explained in our text is that which covers the whole experience of New Birth through Ascension Life, and spans not only time but eternity. "In the ages to come ...."

The only basis of our great salvation now is "the grace of God", and the only glory of the Church, to be on display in the ages to come, will be that of "the exceeding riches of his grace in his kindness toward us through Christ Jesus". We could never have deserved or merited God's favour - there can never be any ground for fleshly glory. May God grant us a fresh revelation of His grace. We would do well to reflect again on the following phrases:

"God, who is rich in mercy";

"His great love wherewith He loved us"
"The exceeding riches of His grace in
His kindness toward us".

GRACE REVEALED IN IMPARTED FAITH

"For by grace are ye saved through faith; and that not of yourselves: it is the gift of God: Not of works, lest any man should boast".

It is grace that saves - but it is faith that appropriates the salvation. There is not one thing that man can do to save himself. Neither his own self-righteousness, nor good works can merit God's salvation. Not even works of faith have any claim to God's salvation. *"By grace (alone) are ye saved".*

The faith, that reaches out and receives salvation, is itself the gift of God's grace. Jesus Himself commanded *"Have faith in God"*, which translates literally as *"Have the faith of God".* (Mark 11:22). In other words, He was exhorting His disciples to take what was available and being offered freely to them.

Paul declares that *"God hath dealt to every man the measure of faith".* (Rom.12:3), and in Romans 10:17 he says, *"Faith cometh by hearing, and hearing (of understanding) by the word of God".* With every unfolding of the Word of God to our understanding by the Holy Spirit comes faith. What we do with that faith is our responsibility. We can either 'sit on it' or we can release it.

We release the faith, that God imparts by His grace, when we accept, believe and act upon what is revealed. Thus, when a sinner comes to Christ through the conviction of the Spirit, he sees his need of salvation and on having his eyes opened to Christ as his only Saviour, he simply believes and receives Him, confessing faith in Him and committing his life to Him.

Thus it is with the whole of this great salvation. As enlightenment comes to our understanding, that by His grace we are made alive together with Him, raised together with Him and seated together in the heavenlies in Christ, so we release our God-given faith and enter into the fulness of our inheritance. This is what must have prompted Charles Wesley *to write:*

> *"Finish then Thy new creation,*
> *Pure and spotless may we be;*
> *Let us see our whole salvation*
> *Perfectly secured by Thee"*

GRACE DEMONSTRATED IN TRANSFORMED LIVING

"For we are his workmanship, created in Christ Jesus unto good works, which God hath before ordained ...." Good works are not the basis of our salvation, but they are the product of it.

The word 'created' is again in the aorist tense and may be translated - 'having been created' in Christ Jesus. As the new creation, in God's thought it is already an accomplished fact. It is already wrought in Christ.

Often the lives of God's redeemed people do not match up to the full transformation purposed beforehand by God. This is because many people have not come to see yet, how God has both purposed and provided for this in His grace. Thus does Charles Wesley plead - "Let us see our whole salvation". With the seeing of it, faith comes to enable us to appropriate it. The more we see and appropriate, the more we are brought into the experience spoken of by the apostle Paul to the Corinthians - "But we all, with open face beholding as in a glass the glory of the Lord, are changed into the same image from glory to glory, even as by the Spirit of the Lord". (2 Cor.3:18).

11. Wherefore remember, that ye being in time past Gentiles in the flesh, who are called Uncircumcision by that which is called the Circumcision in the flesh made by hands;

12. That at that time ye were without Christ, being aliens from the commonwealth of Israel, and strangers from the covenants of promise, having no hope, and without God in the world:

13. But now in Christ Jesus ye who sometimes were far off are made nigh by the blood of Christ.

14. For he is our peace, who hath made both one, and hath broken down the middle wall of partition between us;

15. Having abolished in his flesh the enmity, even the law of commandments contained in ordinances; for to make in himself of twain one new man, so making peace;

16. And that he might reconcile both unto God in one body by the cross, having slain the enmity thereby;

17. And came and preached peace to you which were afar off, and to them that were nigh.

18. For through him we both have access by one Spirit unto the Father

19. Now therefore ye are no more strangers and foreigners, but fellowcitizens with the saints, and of the household of God;

20. And are built upon the foundation of the apostles and prophets, Jesus Christ himself being the chief corner stone;

21. In whom all the building fitly framed together groweth unto an holy temple in the Lord:

22. In whom ye also are builded together for an habitation of God through the Spirit.

CHAPTER 4

THE UNITY OF THE SPIRIT
(Ephesians 2:11–22)

1. THE CHURCH'S BACKGROUND　　　　　(2:11–12)

   The Circumcision and the Uncircumcision
   Israel's Uniqueness
   Gentiles' Alienation

2. THE CHURCH – CHRIST'S BODY　　　　(2:13–18)

   Reconciliation of Gentiles to God by the Cross
   Reconciliation of Gentiles to Israel by the Cross
   Reconciliation of both Israel and Gentiles to God
   Reconciliation effected by the Holy Spirit

3. THE CHURCH – GOD'S TEMPLE　　　　(2:19–22)

   The Political Life of the Church
   The Foundation of the Church
   The Upbuilding of the Church
   The Purpose of the Church

CHAPTER 4

THE UNITY OF THE SPIRIT

1   THE CHURCH'S BACKGROUND   (2:11-22)

THE CIRCUMCISION AND THE UNCIRCUMCISION

"Wherefore remember, that YE being in time past Gentiles in the flesh, who are called Uncircumcision by that which is called the Circumcision ...."

The concept of the Uncircumcision and the Circumcision, the Gentiles and the Jews, You and Us, had occupied much of the apostle's thought. The uniqueness of the Children of Israel as a nation apart from all other nations, both historically and theologically, had captivated Paul's mind all his life. It took a special visitation and revelation of the risen, ascended Christ to change this thinking.

Historically, in the purpose of God, it had to be so, God made a **Covenant of Promise** with Abraham *(Gen.17:2)* and commanded it to be sealed by the sign of circumcision in all the male descendants of his seed.

It was revealed that his son, Isaac, (the child of promise) would be in the line, in which the Covenant of Promise would be fulfilled. *(Gen.17:15-19).*

Later Isaac blessed his son Jacob and confirmed the Covenant that God had made with Abraham *(Gen.28:1-4).* At Bethel God revealed Himself to Jacob in a dream and Himself confirmed to Jacob the Covenant that He had made with Abraham. *(Gen.28:10-19).*

Subsequent to this came Jacob's dramatic experience at Peniel, where he wrestled with the angel of the Lord and prevailed, and where he was given the new name ISRAEL - meaning *"Prince".* * In him

---

* "Israel" - means a little more than just "prince". The verb from which this word is derived, means "to have power/to have power as a prince, i.e. to rule, but there is more - the idea of struggling. It also means

58

and in his posterity was the Abrahamic Covenant of Promise confirmed, until the Covenant was fulfilled in the advent of the Promised One - Christ. *(Gal.3:7-18)*.

Only after it was revealed to him that the Abrahamic Covenant was already fulfilled in Christ, the promised Messiah, did the apostle Paul, as a circumcised Israelite, lose his insular nationalistic and spiritual pride. *(Phil.3:4-6)*. After his conversion to Christianity, the apostle Paul, when making his defence before King Agrippa, spoke clearly of the hope of the promise to which all twelve tribes of Israel still hoped to come - which, of course, he assuredly declared was already fulfilled in Christ. *(Acts 26:5-7)*.

Thus he no longer boasted in his heritage, neither his Judaism, Pharisaism nor circumcision and counted them "but dung, that I may win Christ, And be found in Him ...." *(Phil.3:7-9)*. In identifying himself, therefore, with all who are "in Christ", both Jew and Gentile, he declared, "For we are the circumcision, which worship God in the Spirit ...." *(Phil.3:3)*.

However, the apostle is most lucid and descriptive in this unfolding of vital truth and uses the language understood by his contemporaries. He says - "Ye being in time past Gentiles in the flesh", i.e. ta ethnē meaning - 'the nations', 'ethnic peoples', "who are called the Uncircumcision by that which is called the Circumcision ...."

To Paul, as to all of Israel, this mark of distinction had been exceedingly important, enabling him to elaborate on the true nature of the background of the people to whom he was ministering at that time. For until the fulfilment of the Covenant of Promise in the finished work of Christ the Messiah, Redeemer, Deliverer and Saviour, it was no idle boast to declare oneself a circumcised Israelite. David referred to the giant Goliath as "this uncircumcised Philistine". *(1 Sam.17:36)*. Even Jesus Himself was taken, when

---

"to strive, contend, struggle, persist, persevere". Therefore, it can be translated "he struggles/strives with God", or even, "he rules with God". (D.G.).

eight days old, for the fulfilling of the rite of circumcision. (Luke 2:21).

Thus the apostle is bold to declare *"to the Jew first, and also to the Greek". (Rom.1:16). "We first trusted in Christ. In whom you also trusted, after that ye heard ...." (Eph.1:12,13).*

ISRAEL'S UNIQUENESS

"That at that time ye were without Christ, being aliens from the commonwealth of Israel, and strangers from the covenants of promise ...."

The apostle Paul, himself an Israelite, declared that he had great heaviness and continual sorrow in his heart. He could wish that he himself were accursed from Christ for his brethren, his kinsmen according to the flesh - "Who are Israelites; **to whom pertaineth the adoption, and the glory, and the covenants, and the giving of the Law, and the service of God, and the promises;** Whose are **the fathers,** and of whom as concerning the flesh Christ came, who is over all, God blessed for ever. Amen". *(Rom.9:4,5).*

It is important to note the unique position of the nation of Israel amongst all other nations in the purpose of God. The apostle Paul was most aware of this and also makes particular reference to it elsewhere. (e.g. *Rom.1:16; 3:1,2).* Note the emphasis he gives to the following:

ADOPTION. "To whom pertaineth the adoption". Kenneth Wuest translates that - "Who are possessors of the position of a son by having been placed as such". The word used, of course, is exactly the same word as that in *Eph.1:5.* Of all the nations in the earth God chose Israel as a special people to Himself. Clear references to this are to be found in *Exod.19:5; Psalm 105:6,43; Isa.43:20,21).*

THE GLORY. "Then a cloud covered the tent of the congregation, and the glory of the Lord filled the tabernacle". *(Exod.40:34).* This Glory was special to Israel. This was the Glory that filled the house of the Lord at the dedication of Solomon's Temple. *(2 Chron.5:11-14).*

THE COVENANTS. God made special Covenants with Abraham (Gen.15:7,18), with Isaac (Gen.17:19), with Jacob (Gen.28:13), with the Israelites as a nation (Exod.6:4; 19:5), and with David (2 Sam.23:5). With no other nation did God make such special covenants. Thus the very Scriptures themselves are called 'The Testaments' or 'The Covenants'.

THE LAW. The Covenant that God made with Israel, i.e. the Old Covenant, was of course a Covenant of Law. (Exod.19:3-20:18).

THE SERVICE OF GOD. This translates the word – latreia, which is the word specifically used of spiritual service. This is the service of the priest in the service of God in the sanctuary. Examples of the use of this word are to be seen in Rom.12:1; Heb.9:6; 10:11. This was the service in the sanctuary to which God appointed Aaron and his sons. (Exod.28:1-4; 40:11-16).

THE PROMISES. The apostle Paul is very quick to point out to the Galatians that before God ever made a Covenant of Law with Moses, He made a Covenant of Promise with Abraham. (Gal.3:16-18). There was not only a Covenant of Promise but, as in our text, Eph.2:12, covenants of promise. Thus God spoke through the prophets as in Jer.31:33, Ezek.36:25-27.

THE FATHERS. The Israelites were very proud of their heritage. God had spoken throughout the Scriptures constantly making reference to the Fathers. To Moses He said – "I am the God of thy Fathers, the God of Abraham, the God of Isaac, and the God of Jacob". (Exod.3:6). Stephen, the first Christian martyr, referred to Abraham as "our father" (Acts 7:2) and to all his ancestors, the patriarchs as "our fathers" (Acts 7:11,12). To Jesus, the Pharisees proudly claimed "our fathers did eat manna in the desert" (John 6:31). It is quite evident therefore that the Jews were conscious of having a most special and unique heritage.

CHRIST. "Of whom .... Christ came". God said to Abraham, "And in thy seed shall all the nations of the earth be blessed". (Gen.22:18). Abraham's son was Isaac and his son was Jacob. Jacob was the father of the nation of Israel in whose line of posterity came the Lord Jesus Christ. The apostle Paul, writing to the Galatians, said that this promised seed was Christ Himself. (Gal.3:16). This is exactly what Jesus meant when speaking to the woman of Samaria. "salvation is of the Jews". (John 4:22).

GENTILES' ALIENATION

"Wherefore remember, that ye being in time past Gentiles in the flesh, who are called Uncircumcision by that which is called the Circumcision .... That at that time ye were without Christ, being aliens from the commonwealth of Israel, and strangers from the covenants of promise, having no hope, and without God in the world".

This is the picture portrayed by one who had been steeped in Judaism. There was a clear mark of distinction between Israelites and Gentiles and unless we see, that this racial and spiritual pride was deeply embedded in the hearts and minds of all who were brought up in Judaism, it will be difficult for us to understand the conflict of conscience by which many in the early church were affected.

In Acts 10, when the call came to Peter to involve himself with Gentile people in the house of Cornelius in Caesarea, God had to give him a very disturbing and challenging vision, before he could even think of moving outwith his past traditions. Although the vision, that Jesus had left with the apostles, embraced all people to the uttermost ends of the earth, it was still difficult for Peter to see how such a thing could be accomplished.

To all Judaists, those outwith their religion were considered as uncircumcised, corrupt, Godless, unclean and outside the pale of divine blessing. God had already begun a mighty work of grace in Peter however, for when he arrived at the house of Cornelius he said - "Ye know how that it is an unlawful thing for a man that is a Jew to keep company, or come unto one of another nation; but God hath shewed me that I should not call any man common or unclean". (Acts 10:28). Again, when he preached to this Gentile company for the first time, Peter opened his mouth and said, - "Of a truth I perceive that

God is no respecter of persons". (Acts 10:34).

However, in spite of all the blessing, the power, the working and moving of the Holy Spirit in that situation, as recorded in Acts 10:44-48, his apostolic brethren at Jerusalem contended with him and accused him, saying - "Thou wentest in to men uncircumcised, and didst eat with them". (Acts 11:3).

The apostle Paul, referring to carnal thinking about these things, said that if anyone had cause to have confidence in the flesh, arising from one's Judaistic background, he himself perhaps had more cause than any other and describes this proud boast in Phil.3:4-6, but thankfully ends by saying - "What things were gain to me, those I counted loss for Christ .... and do count them but dung, that I may win Christ, And be found in him ...."

Gentiles, on the other hand, had no claims to such a heritage. They were aliens, as far as the commonwealth of Israel was concerned. They were strangers from the Covenants of Promise that God had made with Israel. They were without hope and without God in this world.

2 THE CHURCH - CHRIST'S BODY (2:13-18)

This is where the Cross figures uniquely, even exclusively in the apostle's vision. In God's purpose of bringing salvation, restoration and reconciliation to men, in Judaism itself with its Old Covenant there could be no basis. The answer lay only in the Cross of our Lord Jesus Christ.

RECONCILIATION OF GENTILES TO GOD BY THE CROSS

"But now in Christ Jesus ye who sometimes were far off are made nigh by the blood of Christ". Thus, at the heart of all the apostle's basic ministry stands the Cross.

*To the **Romans** the apostle says - "Whom God hath set forth to be a propitiation through faith in his blood". (Rom.3:25). This means that the righteousness of a holy God had been satisfied in respect of sin by the atoning blood of Christ.*

*To the **Corinthians** the apostle declares - "We*

preach Christ crucified, unto the Jews a stumbling-block, and unto the Greeks (or Gentiles) foolish-ness; But unto them which are called, both Jews and Greeks, Christ the power of God, and the wisdom of God". (1 Cor.1:23,24).

To the **Galatians** he writes - "O foolish Galatians, who hath bewitched you, that ye should not obey the truth, before whose eyes Jesus Christ hath been evidently (or openly) set forth, crucified among you". (Gal.3:1).

To the **Philippians** he writes - "Let this mind be in you, which was also in Christ Jesus: Who humbled himself, and became obedient unto death, even the death of the cross". (Phil.2:5-8).

To the **Colossians** the apostle writes - "And, having made peace through the blood of his cross, by him to reconcile all things unto himself; .... And you, that were sometime alienated and enemies in your mind by wicked works, yet now hath he reconciled In the body of his flesh through death, to present you holy and unblameable and unreprovable in his sight". (Col.1:20-22).

Thus the apostle Paul clearly sees that the only basic remedy for the Gentiles being reconciled to God, is the Cross of our Lord Jesus Christ.

RECONCILIATION OF GENTILES TO ISRAEL BY THE CROSS

"For he is our peace, who hath made both one, and hath broken down the middle wall of partition between us; Having abolished in his flesh the enmity, even the law of commandments contained in ordinances; for to make in himself of twain one new man, so making peace".

There was no real peace between Israel and the Gentiles. The word for 'middle wall' is mesotoichon, and the word for 'partition' is phragmou. This is a 'fence' or a 'hedge-side path', a 'parting fence'. It is the word used in Matthew 21:33, when Jesus, speaking of the householder who planted a vineyard, hedged it round about. So the middle wall of partition not only kept them from one another, but enclosed them each in their own respective spheres. This permitted of no fellowship, no inter-communion. Judaism was bound with its Old Covenant. Gentiles were a godless mixture of peoples left to their own devices, alienated, separated and strangers from God and His people.

There was not, however, merely division and separatism. **There was enmity.** Under the Old Covenant there was no basis whatsoever for reconciliation, for the Law had its "handwriting of ordinances that was against us, which was contrary to us". (Col.2:14). Now, says the apostle Paul to the Ephesians, He has "abolished in his flesh the enmity, even the law of commandments contained in ordinances; for to make in himself of twain one new man, so making peace". The word katargēsas means 'He has rendered null and void', or 'has abrogated', or 'rendered inoperative', the law of commandments in ordinances. For in no way could the Law be a basis of reconciliation between Jew and Gentile, nor was it ever intended to be so.

Thus, we are completely and exclusively directed not to another system, but to **Christ** Himself. "For **He** is our peace". "Having abolished in **His flesh**". "To make **in Himself** of twain". Verse sixteen emphatically declares that it is the Cross that slays the enmity between Israel and the Gentiles. So the only basis of reconciliation between Jew and Gentile is the Cross of our Lord Jesus Christ.

RECONCILIATION OF BOTH ISRAEL AND GENTILES TO GOD

"And that he might reconcile both unto God in one body by the cross, having slain the enmity thereby: And came and preached peace to you which were afar off, and to them that were nigh".

God's ultimate purpose was not merely to one nation alone. "God so loved the **world**, that he gave his only begotten Son". God's Covenant of Promise, which was to be consummated in His Son, was made before His Covenant of Law and supersedes it in every way. **Law** was God's provision for a time. The Covenant of Promise was forever. Christ and His Cross are the fulfilment of that Covenant. By the Cross was established the New Covenant. The New Testament (Covenant) was in His blood. (Luke 22:20). Now, the only basis of acceptance by a holy God, of both Jews and Gentiles, is faith in the blood of Christ alone.

65

The apostle Paul, when in conflict with Peter, accused him of compromising the simplicity of faith in Christ and His cross with the works of the law as the basis of righteousness. In recalling this incident, he said to the Galatians - *"We who are Jews by nature, and not sinners of the Gentiles, Knowing that a man is not justified by the works of the law, but by the faith of Jesus Christ, ... I am crucified with Christ: .... for if righteousness come by the law, then Christ is dead in vain". (Gal.2:15-21).*

In his Judaism the apostle Paul had been zealous, proud, boastful, antagonistic and an enemy of Christ and His followers, but now he declares - *"God forbid that I should glory, save in the cross of our Lord Jesus Christ". (Gal.6:14).* Thus the Cross, that reconciles Jew and Gentile together, reconciles both in one body to God.

It is at this point that the apostle Paul introduces the real burden of his heart, i.e. the vision concerning the *"Church, which is His Body"*. We can see this by his references to *"**one** new man"*, *"**one** body"*. In chapter 4 of the epistle we will see that the purpose of God is to bring the Body of Christ *"unto a **perfect man**, unto the measure of the stature of the fulness of Christ".*

RECONCILIATION EFFECTED BY THE HOLY SPIRIT

"For through him we both have access by one Spirit unto the Father". Everything that our Lord Jesus Christ accomplished for us in His finished work by the Cross, becomes a reality in the believer's life only as it is applied by the Spirit of God. This is why the blood of Christ is as efficacious to-day, as it was when it was shed on the Cross of Calvary.

The writer to the Hebrews declared - *"By his own blood he entered in once into the holy place, having obtained eternal redemption for us. For if the blood of bulls and of goats, and the ashes of an heifer sprinkling the unclean, sanctifieth to the purifying of the flesh: How much more shall the blood of Christ, who through the eternal Spirit offered himself without spot to God, purge your conscience from dead works to serve the living God?". (Heb.9:12-14).*

It was by the Holy Spirit that our Lord Jesus Christ offered Himself *"without spot to God".* It is that same Holy Spirit who takes of the blood of Christ and applies it to the believer's heart. Whether the believer is Jewish or Gentile there is no difference. Through the blood of Christ we are all reconciled to God and by the same blood we are reconciled to one another. This is the basis of all ministry concerning the Body of Christ. "Christ loved the Church, and gave himself for it".

Thus, only by the Holy Spirit are all the things of Christ made real to the believer. The blessings, that are ours in Christ, are called 'spiritual' blessings, because only by the Spirit of God operating in our spirits can we enter into them and appropriate them. The law of the Spirit is the law of **"life in Christ Jesus"**, says the apostle in Romans 8. Only by the Holy Spirit can we enter into the fulness of the blessing of Christ's finished work. It is the Holy Spirit who is the executor of Christ on earth.

3 THE CHURCH - GOD'S TEMPLE (2:19-22)

THE POLITICAL LIFE OF THE CHURCH

"Now therefore ye are no more strangers and foreigners, but fellowcitizens with the saints, and of the household of God".

The accent now is on reconciliation. Gentiles had been aliens and strangers, without hope and without God. Now they are no more strangers and sojourners but fellowcitizens - sumpolitai - from sun meaning 'together with' - and politēs - 'citizen' - from which our word 'politics' is derived. We are bound up together in a fellow-citizenship of a non-earthly kind. "Our conversation (or political life) is in heaven; from whence also we look for the Saviour, the Lord Jesus Christ". (Phil.3:20). God does not recognise divisions in the Church. His Church is one Church. All those who are in Christ reconciled to God by the Spirit through the blood of His Cross, are reconciled to each other and all are bound together, committed together, united together with the saints, and of the household of God. All are part of God's family, His household.

In such fellowship there is sharing with one

another, caring for one another, submission to one another, commitment to one another. We share together the very life of the Lord. In Communion we experience what the apostle Paul declared, "The cup of blessing which we bless, is it not the communion of the blood of Christ?" (1 Cor.10:16). We share and experience together, in fellowship and in all our relationships, the cleansing power of the blood of Christ. "But if we walk in the light, as he is in the light, we have fellowship one with another, and the blood of Jesus Christ his Son cleanseth us from all sin". (1 John 1:7). And "the bread which we break, is it not the communion of the Body of Christ? For we being many are one bread and one body". (1 Cor.10:16-17). We share together the life of the Lord - His life in us. This is the fellowship - (koinōnia) - that God has purposed for His people.

THE FOUNDATION OF THE CHURCH

"And are built upon the foundation of the apostles and prophets, Jesus Christ Himself being the chief corner stone".

How do we understand this in the light of these words? - "For other foundation can no man lay than that is laid, which is Jesus Christ". (1 Cor.3:11). In Matthew 16:15-18 Jesus said to the disciples - "But whom say ye that I am? And Simon Peter answered and said, Thou art the Christ, the Son of the living God. And Jesus answered and said unto him, Blessed art thou, Simon Bar-jona: for flesh and blood hath not revealed it unto thee, but my Father which is in heaven. And I say also unto thee, That thou art Peter, and upon this rock I will build my church".

Did Jesus mean that Peter would be the rock on which He would build His Church? What we have come to understand about this important passage is that the rock, upon which the Church is being built, is Christ Himself.*   This was the **revelation** that the

---

* "I believe the verse has many levels: i. The Stone is Christ (as above). ii. The Stone is revealed by our confession of Christ to be the Son of the living God. iii. The "Stone"-man is the man who makes such confession, i.e. Peter and all who like him make such confessions".

(R.W.)

apostle Peter had of Him, when he said - "Thou art the Christ, the Son of the living God". The revelation is of Christ Himself.

Thus it is that the believers, who comprise the Church, are built upon the foundation of the apostles and prophets, Jesus Christ Himself being the chief corner stone. What is the foundation of the apostles and prophets? It is perfectly clear from the text, that it is not in the apostles and prophets that the whole building is fitly framed together: it is in Christ Himself, the chief corner stone. As with Peter, so with the rest of the apostles and prophets. The foundation is the revelation they have received of Christ. If their apostolic and prophetic function is in any way involved in the meaning here, it is only to the degree that they reflect Christ's Apostleship and Prophethood.

In verses 3-6 of the next chapter of the epistle we have the apostle Paul declaring that he had received a dispensation of the grace of God, when, - "by revelation he made known unto me the mystery; .... Which in other ages was not made known unto the sons of men, as it is now revealed unto his holy apostles and prophets by the Spirit; That the Gentiles should be fellowheirs, and of the same body, and partakers of his promise in Christ by the gospel".

This is the foundation. It is based on Christ. In fact, it is a revelation that is completely immersed in Christ. As we saw in Chapter 1 that all the blessings are in the heavenlies in Christ, so now we have this wonderful vision of Christ and His Church: the Gentiles are made "fellowheirs, ... and partakers of His promise in Christ by the gospel".

The analogy of course has been changed from 'body' to 'building'. This is the analogy Jesus Himself used in Matthew 16. In Annandale's Concise Dictionary, we have this definition of corner stone - "The stone which forms the corner of the foundation of an edifice; hence, that which is of the greater importance; that on which any system is founded". There is no conflict, it is just another analogy, because the chief corner stone is the main corner stone from which all the rest of the building, the superstructure takes its line and symmetry.

69

Therefore, no matter who we all are - whether apostles, prophets, evangelists, pastors, teachers or undesignated members, as Peter says - "Ye also as lively stones, are built up a spiritual house, an holy priesthood, to offer up spiritual sacrifices, acceptable to God by Jesus Christ. Wherefore also it is contained in the Scripture, "Behold, I lay in Sion a chief corner stone, ... which the builders disallowed, the same is made the head of the corner". (1 Peter 2:5-7).

THE UPBUILDING OF THE CHURCH

"In whom all the building fitly framed together groweth unto an holy temple in the Lord".

This subject of the upbuilding of the Church figures very predominantly in the apostle Paul's vision. It is not a man-made structure, nor is it carelessly thrown together without forethought. The whole structure has been fore-ordained, conceived in the heart of God in ages past. In no way could the Jews and Gentiles be seen to be one together except by the Cross. In no way can the people of God to-day be joined together in true spiritual harmony except 'by the Cross' and 'in Christ'. It is in Him that the whole building is fitly framed together, Jesus Christ Himself being the chief corner stone.

In the outworking of divine purpose there must be growth, there must be upbuilding. The whole building grows *"unto an holy temple in the Lord"*. Jesus said, - *"I will build my Church; and the gates of hell shall not prevail against it"*. Nothing can stop the building that He has planned. Through carnal eyes we may only see the Church rent asunder by schism, by heresies distressed, but the eyes of our understanding are enlightened and because of this we know *"what is the hope of His calling, and what the riches of the glory of His inheritance in the saints, And what is the exceeding greatness of His power to us-ward who believe"*. What we see through spiritual eyes is the Church that He is to present to Himself. It is *"a glorious Church, not having spot, ... and without blemish"*. The systems of men are crumbling beneath their feet, but what He is building is a glorious thing and in that, through grace, we all have a part. We vitally relate in it and are part of the expression of it.

THE PURPOSE OF THE CHURCH

"In whom ye also are builded together for an habitation of God through the Spirit".

What God did, in instructing Moses to build a tabernacle in the wilderness, was only a shadow of things to come. The writer to the Hebrews says – "We have such an high priest, who is set on the right hand of the throne of the Majesty in the heavens; A minister of the sanctuary, and of the true tabernacle, which the Lord pitched, and not man". (Heb.8:1,2).

Whether the material structure be a tent, as was the Tabernacle in the wilderness, or an edifice of grandeur and splendour, as was Solomon's Temple, is quite irrelevant. No longer is it a material building, nor a humanly devised institution. Christ is building His Church with **living** stones, all of whom are in their right setting in the superstructure. It is **in them** that the Lord Himself dwells by His Spirit.

How utterly important it is for God's people to relate together aright, and they can only relate together aright as they relate to the Lord. He Himself is the chief corner stone. His Temple is holy and God Himself dwells therein. All the members of Christ's Church should ever be aware of His divine presence. "Ye are the temple of the living God; as God hath said, I will dwell in them, and walk in them; and I will be their God, and they shall be my people". (2 Cor.6:16).

1. For this cause I Paul, the prisoner of Jesus Christ for you Gentiles

2. If ye have heard of the dispensation of the grace of God which is given me to you-ward:

3. How that by revelation he made known unto me the mystery; (as I wrote afore in few words,

4. Whereby, when ye read, ye may understand my knowledge in the mystery of Christ)

5. Which in other ages was not made known unto the sons of men, as it is now revealed unto his holy apostles and prophets by the Spirit;

6. That the Gentiles should be fellowheirs, and of the same body, and partakers of his promise in Christ by the gospel:

7. Whereof I was made a minister, according to the gift of the grace of God given unto me by the effectual working of his power.

8. Unto me, who am less than the least of all saints, is this grace given, that I should preach among the Gentiles the unsearchable riches of Christ;

9. And to make all men see what is the fellowship of the mystery, which from the beginning of the world hath been hid in God, who created all things by Jesus Christ;

10. To the intent that now unto the principalities and powers in heavenly places might be known by the church the manifold wisdom of God,

11. According to the eternal purpose which he purposed in Christ Jesus our Lord:

12. In whom we have boldness and access with confidence by the faith of him.

13. Wherefore I desire that ye faint not at my tribulations for you, which is your glory.

CHAPTER 5

STEWARDS OF THE REVELATION

(Ephesians 3:1-13)

1. THE STEWARDSHIP OF THE APOSTLE PAUL   (3:1-7)

        The Basis of his Stewardship
        The Nature of his Stewardship
        The Essence of his Stewardship
        The Function of his Stewardship

2. THE STEWARDSHIP OF THE MEMBERS OF THE BODY
                                          (3:8-13)

        The Understanding of Stewardship
        The Purpose of Stewardship
        The Blessing of Stewardship

CHAPTER 5

STEWARDS OF THE REVELATION

1   THE STEWARDSHIP OF THE APOSTLE PAUL   (3:1-7)

*"For this cause I Paul, the prisoner of Jesus Christ
for you Gentiles ...."* This is repeated again in v.14.
*"For this cause I bow my knees unto the Father of
our Lord Jesus Christ ...."*
'This cause' has gripped him. He is so captivated
by this cause, that he willingly and loyally accepts
his status as a bondslave of Jesus Christ. Such is
his commitment, that he gladly submits to being a
prisoner of Rome with the threat of execution
constantly hanging over his head.

From this point on, the apostle Paul parenthetically
unfolds the cause to which he is now so utterly
devoted and committed, right down to v.13. At v.14
he reintroduces the phrase: *"For this cause I bow
my knees unto the Father of our Lord Jesus Christ".*
The vision, that God has imparted, so absolutely
overwhelms and humbles him, that he finds himself
constantly on his knees communing with the God he
now sees as the Father of our Lord Jesus Christ.

"For this cause" refers back to that which he has
just been unfolding in the previous chapter, i.e. *"The
Church, which is His Body".* The revelation is of *"one
new man"* - His Body of which Christ Himself is the
Head. He uses also the other analogy - The Church
which is being built as *"an holy temple .... for an
habitation of God through the Spirit".* Concerning
this holy temple, Christ Himself is the chief corner
stone. This is the cause to which Paul is now
completely committed and which has made him a bondslave of Jesus Christ.

THE BASIS OF HIS STEWARDSHIP

"If ye have heard of the dispensation of the grace of God which is given me to you-ward".

Before we consider this further, let us note in particular his constant reference now to "You Gentiles", i.e. those outside the commonwealth of Israel. This emphasis - 'other nations' - is made over and over in this same chapter. He is a prisoner of Jesus Christ for the Gentiles. This dispensation of grace, that he has received, is towards the Gentiles. The revelation, which he had received, was "that the Gentiles should be fellowheirs ...." He had received this grace that he should "preach among the Gentiles the unsearchable riches of Christ". Since his conversion, God had taken a thorough dealing with him on his cultural, racial, nationalistic and religious pride.

The apostle Paul, describing his call from the moment he met with Jesus on the Damascus Road, when making his defence before king Agrippa, declared: "Rise, and stand upon thy feet: for I have appeared unto thee for this purpose, to make thee a minister and a witness .... Delivering thee from the people, and from the Gentiles, unto whom now I send thee". (Acts 26:16,17). Also, when recalling his acceptance as an apostle of Jesus Christ by the apostolate at Jerusalem, he said: "They gave to me and Barnabas the right hands of fellowship; that we should go unto the heathen (Gentiles), and they unto the circumcision". (Gal.2:9).

What a remarkable transformation this was in a man who had been so violently opposed to anything outside of Judaism. Now he is filled with the love of God. This love for the Gentile peoples is pouring out from him. Thus, by the time we come to the end of this chapter, we find him praying for these same people, that they too will be filled with this divine love.

Concerning this cause the apostle declares that he had received "the dispensation of the grace of God".

The word 'dispensation' - oikonomia - also means 'administration' or 'stewardship'. The basis of this stewardship is the grace of God. He has come to see that there is no basis for any stewardship in the Church of Jesus Christ outside of grace. Stewardship is characterised by grace, whatever its nature, essence or function, for all is of grace.

This is the abounding grace of God towards us spoken of in the first chapter of the epistle. It is cascading, overflowing grace. The apostle Paul declared: "I am the least of the apostles, that am not meet .... But by the grace of God I am what I am". (1 Cor.15:9,10). And again in our text: "Unto me, who am less than the least of all saints". But, he testifies that he has received "the dispensation (stewardship) of the grace of God".

That is exactly what is the outpouring of the Holy Spirit. It is a dispensation of the grace of God to everyone who will believe and receive. It is a divine conferring and a bestowing of His own favour upon such. Paul is saying that he has received a stewardship of the grace of God when he was given the revelation concerning "the Church, which is His Body". It is this that fits and equips him to fulfil it, because in himself he is nothing.

There is no other basis for a stewardship function in the Body of Christ. Outside of this no member can properly function. "Unto every one of us is given grace according to the measure of the gift of Christ". (Eph.4:7). Therefore, no member of the Body of Christ needs to despair or to feel incapable of fulfilling his or her calling or function. God will not give more responsibility to anyone than the measure of grace necessary to cope with it. If we ourselves are not coping in the ministry, we are going beyond the bounds of what God intended for us, or perhaps we are doing the thing that He has not purposed that we should do. We may well be doing our own thing. That is what Saul of Tarsus did - until he met the Lord Jesus Christ.

THE NATURE OF HIS STEWARDSHIP

"How that by **revelation** he made known unto me the mystery; .... Which in other ages was not made known unto the sons of men, as it is now **revealed** unto his holy apostles and prophets by the Spirit".

This word 'mystery' appears a number of times throughout the epistle. As we observed previously, it means 'a secret knowable only by revelation'. We have also seen that God, in making known unto us the mystery of His **Will** caused His **Grace** to abound toward us. There is no way of understanding the purpose of God in Christ Jesus our Lord apart from the **Grace of God**. Things that have been hid in God in ages past are revealed, made known, "unto his holy apostles and prophets by the Spirit". Unless it is the Holy Spirit who makes the things of Christ known to us, we are in the dark, we cannot understand.

That is why, in v.8 of this chapter, the term "the unsearchable riches of Christ" is used. That does not mean 'unknowable'. The unsearchable riches comes from the idea of not being able to track it out, as in Romans 11:33. We cannot by searching, or by wordly wisdom, or by academic knowledge, or by an intellectual approach, search out God or His divine purpose. "How unsearchable are his judgments, and his ways past finding out". So we have no answers outside of Him. There is no knowledge of any worth of that revelation except that imparted by the Holy Spirit. Thus, with conviction the apostle Paul declares that what has been hid in ages past is "now revealed unto his holy apostles and prophets by the Spirit".

The nature of the stewardship that the apostle Paul has received is that of a special revelation, an unfolding of things never understood before. This was completely new to him, for Judaism had never seen any divine purpose outside of its own scheme and pattern of religion.

We already looked at this subject of enlightenment and revelation by the Spirit of God in Chapter 2 of this book, so we do not need to pursue it further. It is good, however, to remind ourselves that, just as the apostle Paul himself needed the Holy Spirit to bring to him revelation and insight into the purpose of God, so do we. "The natural man receiveth not the things of the Spirit of God: for they are foolishness unto him: neither can he know them, because they are spiritually discerned". (1 Cor.2:14).

THE ESSENCE OF HIS STEWARDSHIP

"That the Gentiles should be fellowheirs, and of the same body, and partakers of his promise in Christ by the gospel".

This brings us on to really sacred ground. Of everything else that the apostle Paul declared - this is the heart of it. In the next verse he says: "Whereof I was made a minister". This is the cause that had captivated him and made him a prisoner. This is the cause for which he bows his knees "unto the Father of our Lord Jesus Christ". Not even the threat of martyrdom itself could turn back the apostle Paul from this tremendous cause.

This revelation had never been made known before, but the germ of truth, like the treasure hidden in the field about which Jesus spoke, was already imparted in the Abrahamic Covenant: "In thee and in thy seed shall all the families of the earth be blessed". The unfolding of it, however, had to wait until the revelation given by the Spirit to the apostles and prophets.

Notice how explicit the apostle Paul is about the Gentiles. He calls them "fellowheirs". The word used is sunklēronoma - from sun meaning 'together with' and klēronomos - meaning an 'heir' or 'possessor' or 'participant'. Hence we have the idea of a 'fellow participant', a 'participant together with'. The Gentiles are no longer "aliens from the commonwealth of Israel, and strangers from the covenants of promise, having no hope, and without God in the world". They are no longer "strangers and foreigners, but fellowcitizens with the saints, and of the household of God". Every spiritual promise made to Israel is now applicable to all other nations. In that sense, Israel has lost her uniqueness.

Note how the apostle Paul writes to the Romans in chapter 9. "As he saith also to Osee (Hosea), I will call them my people, which were not my people; and her beloved, which was not beloved. And it shall come to pass, that in the place where it was said unto them, Ye are not my people; there shall they be called the children of the living God .... the Gentiles, which followed not after righteousness, have attained to righteousness, ... which is of faith".

Again in Romans 11 he is answering the question, "I say then, Hath God cast away his people?" He replies in v.11: "Have they stumbled that they should fall? God forbid: but rather through their fall salvation is come unto the Gentiles, for to provoke them to jealousy". The apostle Paul pleaded that we should not be ignorant of this mystery, lest we should be wise in our own conceit - "that blindness in part is happened to Israel, until the fulness of the Gentiles be come in". It is for this reason that the apostle Paul declares: "There is no difference between the Jew and the Greek: for the same Lord over all is rich unto all that call upon him". (Rom.10:12). Again, "God hath concluded them all in unbelief, that he might have mercy upon all". (Rom.11:32).

Can we see what this did for the apostle Paul? Now the world was at his feet. Every nation was before him. God had a message of hope for all men. All the privileges, previously available to Israel as a nation, were now widely available to all who should believe, of every nation, tribe and tongue.

"And of the same body". The words "same body" translate the Greek word - sussōma - meaning 'united together in the same body".

This is why he uses the language of "one new man", "one body". No more does the middle wall of partition exist between Jew and Gentile. This has been broken down in Christ, and by the blood of Christ all who are afar off have been made nigh to God. He made of the two "one new man, so making peace". Both now have equal access in one body "by one Spirit unto the Father".

Only through grace, by the pouring out of the Spirit of God, could Saul of Tarsus have been transformed into a mighty apostle for the Gentiles, for the nations of the world. It would have been utterly impossible for him to have given himself in such an utterly surrendered way, completely unreservedly, wholly submissive to the Lordship of Christ, had he not received the revelation of Christ in His Church; this one Church that comprised not only Jews, but Gentiles as well. The apostle is immersed in this revelation and enthralled with it.

Is not this what the Spirit of God is seeking to do in these days? There are so many factions, there is still so much strife, there are so many divisions, so much disparity between one group and another, so much self-seeking, self-will, self-assertiveness: truly, so much that is of the flesh. What men have been originating and organising, has made the Church look - just as has been described in the hymn: "By schism rent asunder, by heresies distressed".

What then is the vision for the hour? It is the vision that Paul had, that "the Church which is His body" is **One Church,** *and that all should be united together in the same body. What does it matter if people worship God in different ways, as long as they recognise that, by the blood of Christ, in heart and in spirit they belong together; that every member in the body of Christ belongs together; that each one essentially relates together and should be seen to co-ordinate with each other? Then, the attitudes, motives and behaviour of all involved will manifest the loveliness of the fruit of the Spirit - love, joy, peace, longsuffering, gentleness, goodness, meekness, faith and self-control.*

"And partakers of his promise in Christ by the gospel". The word for 'partakers' is summetocha - meaning 'fellow-partaker', or 'partaker together with'. Thus, the promise of God in Christ by the gospel is no longer the sole possession of the Jewish nation. This belongs to all nations in Christ. In Galatians 3:16 the apostle points out that the seed of promise is Christ Himself. In Him all nations of the earth are blessed. And finally the apostle says: "And if ye be Christ's, then are ye Abraham's seed, and heirs according to the promise". (Gal.3:29).

What an emphasis the Holy Spirit has put on the unity of the body in this beautiful verse. All three phrases, **"fellowheirs",** **"same body".** **"partakers",** *have that little preposition 'sun' as a prefix, meaning that the emphasis in this one verse alone is threefold - 'together with', 'together with', 'together with'. How can we ignore this? If our hearts and minds remain open, the Holy Spirit will reveal clearly the importance of this vision and we will be captivated by it, as was the apostle Paul over nineteen centuries ago.*

THE FUNCTION OF HIS STEWARDSHIP

Concerning this cause, this ministry, this vision, said the apostle Paul, "I was made a minister, according to the gift of the grace of God given unto me by the effectual working of his power". The word 'ministry' here translates the word diakonos - which means 'one who renders service to another'. For this ministry, the apostle Paul had received a gift of the grace of God imparted by the power of the Holy Spirit. Only by the effectual working of the Holy Spirit's power is anyone truly equipped for the fulfilling of the ministry to which he has been called of God.

2 THE STEWARDSHIP OF THE MEMBERS OF THE BODY

(3:8-13)

THE UNDERSTANDING OF STEWARDSHIP

"Unto me, who am less than the least of all saints, is this grace given, that I should preach among the Gentiles the unsearchable riches of Christ. And to make all men see what is the fellowship of the mystery".

As already mentioned, the word 'unsearchable' literally means 'the track, which cannot be explored', hence 'inscrutable', 'incomprehensible'. However are people going to come to a knowledge of the riches in Christ if these are inscrutable, incomprehensible?

It is the natural mind that cannot understand the things of God. "Christ crucified, unto the Jews a stumblingblock, and unto the Greeks foolishness; But unto them which are called, both Jews and Greeks, Christ the power of God, and the wisdom of God". (1 Cor.1:23,24). This is why it is so utterly essential that preachers, teachers and ministers of the Gospel should be anointed by the Spirit of God. How else can the Word of God come alive to the people? In what other way can things, incomprehensible to the natural mind, be understood by it. Only by an anointed ministry of the Word can the things of Christ be revealed, received, and understood by the human mind.

In the ministry, the burden on the heart of the apostle Paul was that he should "make all men see what is the fellowship of the mystery". That word 'fellowship', which translates koinōnia, is now generally accepted by all the Bible Societies, in the light of more evidence, as being the word oikonomia, which was used in v.2, and means 'stewardship', or 'administration'. This does not rob it of the beauty of what is meant by fellowship, but rather gives it more force and meaning. This brings home to every member of the Body the nature and responsibility of that fellowship. Not only has the apostle Paul been given a stewardship by the grace of God, but everyone, involved in the Body of Christ, has likewise received a stewardship from the Lord.

It was not sufficient that the apostle Paul had received a stewardship of the grace of God concerning the revelation of the unity of the Church as the Body of Christ. He was well aware in his calling, that he had the responsibility of making all men see what is their stewardship of this mystery. As the revelation brought an awareness of responsibility to the apostle, so it is with all to whom revelation is given. It is not enough to receive light, but we must go on to walk in that light. It was not enough that the apostle Paul should disclose the mystery, making known that "which from the beginning of the world hath been hid in God". It was exceedingly important that all men understand the stewardship of the light received about this revelation.

Thus, to everyone in the Body of Christ who understands this truth, there comes the responsibility of relating aright to each other brother and sister in the Body. Certainly, God sets the members in the Body as it pleases Him, and the Lord calls us to faithfulness in our setting. Let us be faithful where God has put us. As we mingle, however, amongst our brothers and sisters everywhere, in every branch of the Christian Church, let us permit no relationship barriers. Rather, by the grace of God let the barriers that hinder fellowship be pulled down, so that all will feel the love of God poured out upon them. No matter the attitudes of others - all should feel the grace of God flowing out from those whose eyes have been opened. It is in this way that the enlightened will bear faithfully the responsibility of their stewardship. This is how people will become aware of unity in the Body of Christ.

This is exactly what Jesus prayed for in John 17:21 "That they all may be one; as thou, Father, art in me, and I in thee, that they also may be one in us: that the world may believe that thou hast sent me". Surely the world is yet to see Christ revealed through the Church. This is what the Church is called to be: the manifestation of "the fulness of him that filleth all in all".

Just as the human body needs every member set in its proper place, properly co-ordinated together and joined to its head, so that it functions - every part of it, in proper submission to the head; so does the Body of Christ need to be aware of the responsibility of its stewardship and to discharge it well in the grace of God.

When we come to chapter 4 of the epistle we will see that God has given this stewardship responsibility not only to the apostles and prophets and other ministers, but also to every member. However, although every member of the Body has a function and a ministry, there are many who simply do not want to know. Some prefer to leave it all to the ecclesiastical hierarchy. But God has called all the saints to be a corporate body, a royal priesthood, to "shew forth the praises of him who hath called you out of darkness into his marvellous light". On reflection, this is the way the apostle Paul prayed for the whole Church, that all should receive "the spirit of wisdom and revelation in the knowledge of him", that the eyes of everyone's heart would be enlightened.

Jesus said, "For unto whomsoever much is given, of him shall be much required". (Luke 12:48). Therefore, what we have received from God, we must impart to others. We receive blessing to dispense it. We receive light to walk in light. And, for this purpose, to everyone has been given "grace according to the measure of the gift of Christ". This is the grace that will radiate from us, as we mingle amongst the Lord's people. In this grace we will have the right word for the right time. More - our very presence will communicate something as we faithfully, lovingly and willingly discharge the responsibility of this - our stewardship. People will become aware of God in an atmosphere charged by His living presence.

THE PURPOSE OF STEWARDSHIP

"To the intent that now unto the principalities and powers in the heavenlies might be known by the Church the manifold wisdom of God". The Church is the visible expression of the fulness of Christ on earth. But this is not all. It is also the visible expression of "the manifold wisdom of God" even to the 'rulers', and to 'the authorities' in the heavenlies.

Some people convey the idea that these are all good angelic powers. The words used, however, are exactly the same as in Ephesians 1;20 and Ephesians 6:12, where, in each of these cases, the words "In the heavenlies" are used. In the first of these references, both good and evil powers must of necessity be referred to, because all things are said to be under Christ's feet. In the latter case they are clearly evil powers, and the same words are used in the same phrase - en tois epouraniois. Therefore, the Church seated in the heavenlies in Christ, reigning in authority with Him, displays to all principalities and authorities, even to the arch-enemy of our souls, the manifold wisdom, or the many-sided wisdom of God.

In this position in the heavenlies in Christ, the Church shares His reigning authority. The Church is not subject to domination by any powers. The Church submits only to Christ the Lord and with Him shares the total victory and triumph of His finished work. That is why the apostle Paul, in Romans 5, talks about "reign(ing) in life by one, Jesus Christ". And why, in that majestic, inspiring, prophetic, Messianic Psalm 110, the Church is seen to be God's willing people, manifesting forth the Lordship and Priesthood of Christ, as He rules through His Church in the midst of His enemies.

"By the church", translated from the Greek, really means 'by means of the church' or 'through the medium of the church'. It is as the Church comes to know its position in Christ, understands and enters into the revelation of the "One Body", that the manifold wisdom of God is revealed "unto the principalities and powers in the heavenlies". The only way that the Church can fulfil an effective ministry in and to the world, will be as its members clearly grasp their position "in the heavenlies in Christ" and enter into the blessings with which they have been blessed in Him. Then the Church will be a ministry to the world in its darkness, gloom and despair. "Arise, shine; for thy light is come ...."

All this is "According to the eternal purpose which he purposed in Christ Jesus our Lord". No transitory thing this, no passing phase. God's purpose in His Church is an eternal one. The Church will forever display the wonder and glory of the grace of God.

THE BLESSING OF STEWARDSHIP

"In whom we have boldness and access with confidence by the faith of him". The word for 'boldness' has the idea of confidence and assurance, particularly to do with speaking. It comes from the word meaning 'a speech'. And the word for 'access' simply means 'the approach', or 'admission'.

All of this, says the apostle Paul, is in Him, in Christ Jesus our Lord, in whom is vested all the eternal purposes of God for the ages. It speaks clearly of confidence and blessing, that comes through being in right relationship with Him through grace. But there must surely be some reference here to the ministry in which the apostle has been so involved, concerning which he enjoins all the members of the Body of Christ to be likewise fully involved. All of it is "in Christ Jesus our Lord". Even the faith, which brings the trust and the confidence, is "the faith of the Son of God, who loved us and gave himself for us".

To be walking in the centre of God's will, to be fulfilling the ministry that God has committed to us, to discharge our stewardship faithfully and responsibly - is to live continuously in the blessing of the Lord.

"Wherefore I desire that ye faint not at my tribulations for you, which is your glory". The suffering and tribulations, testings and trials and afflictions of the apostle Paul were not to be an occasion for faint-heartedness on the part of the believers. He himself was in blessing. His joy was in fulfilling the will of God and faithfully discharging his stewardship. This ministry, with all its sacrifices, was particularly for them, for God had commissioned him as an apostle to the Gentiles.

This was his privilege and opportunity, to be

identified with Christ, to share in "the fellowship of his sufferings".

To the Colossians the apostle writes: "Who now rejoice in my sufferings for you, and fill up that which is behind of the afflictions of Christ in my flesh for his Body's sake, which is the Church". There was a plea in the apostle's heart: "I desire that ye faint not". For him to see the fulfilment of the purpose of God in his life and ministry and in that of the Church, was a cause for great joy and rejoicing. "The sufferings of this present time are not worthy to be compared with the glory which shall be revealed in us". (Rom.8:18).

All of this, of course, was because he lived as every member should "by the faith of the Son of God, who loved us and gave himself for us". (Gal.2:20). It was not his own faith. It was the faith of Him who had become "the author and finisher of our faith; Who for the joy that was set before him endured the cross, despising the shame, and is set down at the right hand of the throne of God". (Heb.12:2).

Ephesians 3:14-21

14. For this cause I bow my knees unto the Father of our Lord Jesus Christ,
15. Of whom the whole family in heaven and earth is named,
16. That he would grant you, according to the riches of his glory, to be strengthened with might by his Spirit in the inner man;
17. That Christ may dwell in your hearts by faith; that ye, being rooted and grounded in love,
18. May be able to comprehend with all saints what is the breadth, and length, and depth, and height;
19. And to know the love of Christ, which passeth knowledge, that ye might be filled with all the fulness of God.
20. Now unto him that is able to do exceeding abundantly above all that we ask or think, according to the power that worketh in us,
21. Unto him be glory in the church by Christ Jesus throughout all ages, world without end. Amen.

CHAPTER 6

RESOURCES OF POWER AND LOVE

(Ephesians 3:14-21)

1. THE ENDUEMENT OF THE SPIRIT   (3:14-16)

        Practical Implications
        Prayerful Devotion
        Paternal Relationship
        Power of the Spirit

2. THE INDWELLING OF CHRIST   (3:17-19)

        Basis of Love
        Stability of Love
        Relationship of Love
        Experience of Love

3. THE GLORY OF GOD   (3:20,21)

        In His Measureless Ability
        In each Individual Member
        In the Corporate Body

CHAPTER 6

RESOURCES OF POWER AND LOVE

1   THE ENDUEMENT OF THE SPIRIT   (3:14-16)

PRACTICAL IMPLICATIONS

"For this cause". This cause has completely captivated the apostle Paul. The unfolding of it brings complications, opposition, misunderstanding, rejection. In the end it will mean possible martyrdom, not only for himself, but for others also who thus commit themselves to God and this new revelation.

Already the apostle Paul has suffered much tribulation, which has adversely affected some of the believers. This is why he appeals to them all not to be fainthearted because of his sufferings.

Having unfolded the vision and shared the burden of his heart concerning the Church, which is the Body of Christ, it is only as the Church comes to understand what are its God-given resources and the power and love available to it, that the 'cause' will be fully realised and the vision fulfilled.

PRAYERFUL DEVOTION

"I bow my knees". Both the vision and the prospect of its fulfilment brings the apostle to his knees. The vision is glorious, even awesome. But to see the fulfilment is a much more practical thing than simply having the vision in one's heart and mind. This involves people who, from varying backgrounds and different levels of maturity, actually belong together and have to learn to relate together in unity. This is not easy, so he prays for them all: "That he would grant you ...." It is vital that the saints receive something more from God, if they are going to live in the good of what is now being revealed.

In these days of the moving of the Holy Spirit amongst the people of God, He is guiding them into

all truth. It is, however, easy to imagine that having
truth revealed to us and thereby coming into an
understanding of it - is, in itself, evidence of the
fact that we are already living in the good of it.
But this is not so. Vision always calls for faith and
active co-operation with God. This we can only know
through vital **prayer** and **communion.** To have vision
alone would, in the end of the day, make us merely
visionary.

Elijah had vision from God and knew exactly what
was the will and purpose of God when, on Mount
Carmel, in the most challenging circumstances, God
sent fire and rain from heaven. It was not enough
for Elijah to know what God wanted - what He had
promised. It was essential that he himself obeyed the
Lord, co-operated with Him, communed with Him and
prayed. It was then that God sent the fire. It was
then that He sent the rain.

The apostle Paul knows full well that in the face
of spiritual conflict, of the hardness of men's hearts,
of the blindness in the hearts and minds of men and
women: there is no way in which this vision he has
received from God can be fulfilled, except through
prayer. "I bow my knees", he says. If we are moved
by vision from God, if we know what God is saying
and doing and purposes to do in these days, we will
be so moved in our hearts that we can do no other
than come to God in vital and close communion.

PATERNAL RELATIONSHIP

"Unto the Father .... Of whom the whole family
...." This can hardly be an irrelevant aside. The
concept of the Fatherhood of God had come to the
apostle Paul only since he had received the
revelation of Jesus Christ as the Son of God. Now
God is his Father, and "in Christ" God is the Father
of the whole redeemed family. That all the family
know their vital relationship to God and to one another
is of paramount importance.

"The whole family" translated literally means
'every family'. Most commentators, therefore, suggest
that the concept in Paul's mind is that God is the
Father of all created life: every species, rank or
order of created beings.

91

While we cannot dismiss this as being irrelevant, it does not seem reasonable to me that the apostle would break away from his main theme and burden, which speaks primarily of the 'whole redeemed family'.

It was Jesus who first made people aware of the Fatherhood of God, when He taught them how to pray "Our Father". To the apostle Paul the uniqueness of God's role as 'Father' was indeed very special. To the Romans he declares: "Ye have received the Spirit of adoption, whereby we cry, Abba, Father .... we are the children of God: And if children, then heirs: heirs of God, and joint-heirs with Christ". (Rom.8:15-17).

No longer does the apostle see a divided family. The God, who is Father of the circumcision, is Father of the uncircumcision also. To see this operating and working out amongst all the different tribes and peoples, who make up this family, is evidence of "the manifold wisdom of God". This brings the apostle to prayer, as it should do amongst all those who constitute the family of God.

POWER OF THE SPIRIT

"To be strengthened with might by his Spirit in the inner man". The word 'might', translated from the Greek, is once again the 'power' spoken of in Acts 1:8. "The inner man" is the spirit of man, where the Holy Spirit dwells. Domestic, social, emotional, racial, cultural problems can easily adversely affect the family relationships. This is why it is not sufficient to have an experience of the Holy Spirit that is understood merely in terms of emotional and physical sensations. The ministry of the Holy Spirit must be in the realm of the spirit, then the emotional and physical feelings can be disciplined and brought into line with what is of God in the spirit.

If charismatic experience is understood in terms merely of an "emotional high" or some such feeling, then this is neither sufficient. nor at all satisfactory. Unless love, joy, peace and all the other aspects of relationships in the family of God, the Body of Christ, are positively the 'fruit of the Spirit'. i.e. the outflowing of the divine life imparted to the spirit of the believers by the dynamic power of the Holy

Spirit, then we may witness a soulish rather than a spiritual manifestation.

This is the primary reason for the emotional instability that characterises so many of God's people. This is the bane of so much of modern pentecostal and charismatic experience. For this reason we need a Word from God, a (rhēma) Word that reveals by the Spirit that which is already recorded for us in holy writ, "For the word of God is quick, and powerful, and sharper than any twoedged sword, piercing even to the dividing asunder of soul and spirit". (Heb.4:12).

Let us not limit God in our 'charismatic experience'. Remember that Jesus promised us dynamic power. Only with this enduement "in the inner man" can we properly and efficiently, fully discharge the responsibility of our stewardship. By the power of the Spirit alone can we relate together as we should in the Body of Christ, thus to stand against the wiles of the devil - and overcome.

Nor should we limit the power at our disposal. The measure of this blessing and power, for which the apostle prayed for us, was not simply 'out of', but 'according to' the riches of His glory.

2 THE INDWELLING OF CHRIST (3:17-19)

BASIS OF LOVE

"That Christ may dwell in your hearts by faith". It is quite inconceivable to have the Holy Spirit strengthen us "in the inner man" without Christ Himself indwelling us. This is the whole object of the Holy Spirit's ministry, i.e. to reproduce the Christ life in us. "The law of the Spirit (is the law) of life in Christ Jesus ...." (Rom.8:2). Thus the life that is in Him is that which indwells the believer by the Spirit.

This can only be realised and appropriated, as with every spiritual experience, "by faith", i.e. our active, willing co-operation and obedience to the Word revealed.

The same thought was in the apostle's heart when he wrote - "I am crucified with Christ: nevertheless I live: yet not I, but Christ liveth in me .... I live

93

by the faith of the Son of God ...." (Gal.2:20).

Even the faith by which we respond and co-operate is an impartation of divine grace. This faith is not our faith - it is "the faith of the Son of God". The life and the strength that is imparted to the inner man by the Spirit is the very Christ - life itself.

This is why the apostle was unequivocal in his affirmation and confession - "Christ liveth in me". Let us all, with the same assurance of faith, without wavering, stand on the truth revealed and enjoy the fulness of the Christ within, for this is what the apostle prayed would be our portion.

STABILITY OF LOVE

"That ye, being rooted and grounded in love ...." i.e. 'strengthened with roots' and 'rendered firm and unwavering in love'.

To have the indwelling Christ within us, is to have His nature too. One cannot have Him without knowing and experiencing His life and love. To have this experience is literally - to be strong in the Lord and in the power of His might. Not to have this as an ongoing experience of the Spirit of God in our lives, is to create instability and inconsistency among us. It is indeed this lack that is the reason for the exposure of such weakness, frailty and tensions in many of the relationships of members of the Body of Christ.

Unless people have come to know this inner strengthening of the Holy Spirit, this empowering of the inner man by the Spirit of God, they will become subject to many things that either incapacitate them, immobilise them or disqualify them from the responsible kind of ministry and service that God has purposed for them.

What are some of these basic things that afflict many of the Lord's people? This is what the apostle Paul refers to as 'walking in the flesh', rather than 'walking in the Spirit', i.e. seeking to live our lives with carnal energy and effort, rather than with the wisdom, light, strength and power imparted to us by the constant infilling of the Holy Spirit. This creates all kinds of personal and relationship problems; producing carnal reactions, feelings of inadequacy and inferiority or even superiority;

bringing about tensions, anxieties, fears, worries and in general, producing an emotional instability that adversely affects the work of God.

To move forward into the fuller experience of relating together and understanding together "with all saints .... the love of Christ, which passeth knowledge", each one of us has to become rooted and grounded in the love of Christ, through the indwelling of Christ Himself, wrought in us by the strengthening power of the Holy Spirit.

All who understand the responsibility of stewardship in the Body of Christ, particularly those with a leadership responsibility, must be people who have been delivered from fleshly attitudes, motives and behaviour. They will be enabled to react to all kinds of situations - not in a carnal or fleshly way. They will find themselves emotionally sound and stable in the midst of all the upheavals of life around them, the conflict that rages and the relationship upsets that are produced by the world, the flesh and the devil.

Such people, in whom the love of Christ dwells, are strong in the Lord and in the power of His might. They are strengthened with roots and rendered firm and unwavering. Come what may, they remain true examples of the Christ life for all to behold and follow.

RELATIONSHIP OF LOVE

"May be able to comprehend with all saints ...." means 'that you may be fully able to understand and perceive, or grasp hold of, together with all the saints'.

Here is a total God-given ability (by the Spirit) to understand, perceive and grasp hold 'together with all the saints' of something exceedingly important - this special, unique Christ-love. Let us erase from our mind the idea that this knowledge of the love of Christ is merely a personal thing, although that is how many of us have beheld it. We have individually looked at the love of Christ and desired to be filled with it. It is, of course, very personal, as is salvation, and as is being filled with the Spirit.

In the context of 'the vision' about which Paul is praying, however, or "this cause" for which he bows his knees "unto the Father" - he sees but one Body. True love has no meaning outside of relationships. Here, Christ's love is seen to pervade the whole Body. It is immersed in His love. The Body of Christ walks, grows and functions in that love, as we shall see in chapter 4 of the epistle. This is the Body ministry, the 'together with all the saints' ministry of love.

This love is really divine. Human love of either the eros - 'sensuous kind', or philos - 'friendship kind', has its limitations. Such love can be self-motivated, inspired or centred. Often it is love for its own sake. The love of Christ - agapē love, is never like that, never merely personal and selfish. It is of the nature of Him who is God. It is His love, and nothing less, in which we should be rooted and rendered firm and unwavering. But there are those who do not understand the true nature of this love.

As we think of the divisions, factions, self-seeking, self-assertiveness, self-will and all other such carnal things that tend to afflict the Body of Christ, it is clearly imperative that all the members are rooted and grounded in this divine love. Otherwise, we will see other people through carnal eyes. Pure, wholesome and binding relationships are impossible without this love of Christ being established within us.

There is no way that the family of God, the Body of Christ, can relate together aright, unless the love of Christ is at the heart of such fellowship. This love is paramount. Sadly, we have tended to put many things before it, such as doctrines, organisations, groupings, denominations, etc.

There was no doubt whatever in the apostle's mind that, without this divine love, the Jewish and Gentile factions would not be able in any way to properly relate together. Judaism would impose its traditions on the new Gentile converts, maybe even look upon them as though in some second-class category. Gentiles, on the other hand, might react in bitterness and anger. There would be carnality, division and strife. In no way could this body be **ONE** - without being bound together in the love of Christ.

EXPERIENCE OF LOVE

"And to know the love of Christ .... with all the fulness of God". There is no possibility of understanding this love by carnal or natural reasoning. That is why there are many problems to this day. This love surpasses knowledge, but it can be known by the experience imparted by the Spirit.

It is not human love with all its carnal limitations. To be filled with this love, to experience this love in its *"breadth, and length, and depth, and height"* with all the people of God, is indeed to be filled with all the fulness of God: for God is love.

Since this love surpasses knowledge, how can we know it? It is just like *"the peace .... which passeth all understanding".* We cannot understand it, but we can know it in our experience. We can have it. That is far more wonderful than being able to have an objective comprehension of it. It is much more meaningful to be immersed in the love and to be experiencing it in a practical way. That is what Paul means here, when he prays that we may know in our very life and experience *"the love .... which passeth knowledge".* This is the only love that will break down all the barriers and unite the Church of God.

This love is the attribute, the aspect of His divine nature, that is the ground upon which God has brought us as members into the Body of Christ. By this He has saved, cleansed and redeemed us. It is all in His grace, His unmerited love and favour. And we cannot understand anything about the fulness of God, without understanding the love of God.

To understand the love of God is to experience and express the nature of that love. When we consider all that Jesus had to face and how God so loved such a rebellious, sinful and utterly degraded humanity: we realise that only His love could have won through, and it did. When we are filled with that kind of love it will inevitably be manifested.

We can talk about the unity of the faith, the oneness of the Body of Christ; but we cannot even begin to conceive of it, apart from the love of God in us, and our being filled with all the fulness of that love.

There is so much about people that mars the unity, so much that is despicable, so much that is unlike Christ. This can be really felt. But when we are filled with this love, only then can we begin to conceive of the Body of Christ being one. En agapē - 'in love' - are two absolutely vital words that come out time and time again. "In love" - we walk in it. We grow in it. We function in it. And it is "in love" that we are able to understand "this cause" for which Paul gives himself wholly to God in prayer.

3 THE GLORY OF GOD (3:20,21)

IN HIS MEASURELESS ABILITY

"Now unto him that is able to do exceeding abundantly above all that we ask or think". - 'But to him who is able above all things to do super-abundantly above what we ask or think' - 'above all that we dare ask or think, or perceive'.

Is the foregoing a mere beautiful ideal, a fanciful dream? Are we being merely idealistic? If we limit any of this to man's own ability or ingenuity, we are simply dreaming.

We would be very naive to imagine that, having caught the vision, there are no serious difficulties. The whole history, of what we call 'the Church', has been fraught with seemingly insurmountable problems. Even now there are lots of clear evidences of obstructions to unity in the Body of Christ. If we did not understand the foregoing, then we would not see an answer to the many problems.

If a few of God's people cannot see fit to agree together, to be one and love each other, how can the whole spectrum of those, who claim to be members of the Body of Christ and who are from one extreme to the other at variance, ever conceive of the Body being seen as one. "We think", and if we think carnally, this is exactly how we will think - the utter impossibility of such a thing ever coming to pass.

That, however, is not the language that expresses this revelation. The gifts of the ascended Christ are given to the Church. "For the perfecting of the saints, for the work of the ministry, for the edifying of the

Body of Christ: Till we ALL come in the unity of the faith, and of the knowledge of the Son of God, unto a perfect man, unto the measure of the stature of the fulness of Christ". (Eph.4:12,13). If this is the divine purpose, then we must surely come to it.

Merely to think about this vision seems to defy our imagination. We are baffled by the very thought. To think much about it may in the end produce thoughts of its utter impossibility, at least in this life. That is why so many people have resigned themselves to the thought that this is something to be realised only in the glory land. For we know that God will be glorified "in the Church by Christ Jesus throughout all ages".

In the 17th chapter of John the prayer of Jesus concerning this very matter is clearly recorded for us. In verse 9 He prays for the disciples whom He had chosen at that time - "for them which thou hast given me". But in verses 20,21 He is praying "for them also which shall believe on me through their word; That they all may be one; as thou, Father, art in me, and I in thee, that they also may be one in us: that the world may believe that thou hast sent me".

We cannot ignore this prayer, nor evade its implications or prophetic insight. This essential oneness of the believers, in and with the persons of the Godhead, for the express purpose of revealing the Son of God who was sent of the Father to an unbelieving world, takes the vision out of the glory land future concept and places it into the here and now, where the Holy Spirit is being poured out upon all flesh.

If we had spent as much time being identified together in the ministry, for which Christ prayed, that the Church might be made perfect in one, as we spent in trying to perpetuate our divisions, then something far more wonderful might have emerged. But it will emerge - for the prayer of Jesus will not go unanswered. The outpouring of the Spirit of God is given for this very reason, that the Church may be seen to be that for which Christ prayed, so that "the world may believe".

However, it will not come about by our own carnal

efforts - He is "able to do exceeding abundantly".
It is God's power, God's ability - no less.

IN EACH INDIVIDUAL MEMBER

"According to the power that worketh (goes on
operating) in us". This is exactly the power about
which Jesus spoke in Acts 1:8. This is the charismatic
experience of which the New Testament is full, and
the charismatic renewal to which millions of believers
all over the world testify in this late twentieth century.

This is the same Holy Ghost power that Paul said
was working effectually and mightily in him by His
grace and that made him "a minister .... to preach
.... the unsearchable riches of Christ; And to make
all men see what is the fellowship (stewardship) of
the mystery". This is the power about which Paul
declared that he was praying, that they would be
strengthened with might .... in the inner man. "The
inner man" means our spirit - for "He that is joined
unto the Lord is one spirit". His Spirit - one with
our spirit. Renewed day by day in the inward man
- i.e. our quickened, awakened, God-conscious part
of us. This is the God-communicating part of us - in
our spirit that disciplines, enlightens, teaches our
mind and renews it, so that it can transform our
whole life.

It is this power of the Holy Spirit operating within
us, that enables us to be and act in a way that we
could not possibly be or do otherwise.

If all God's people could only begin to grasp this
and, "by faith", operate according to the unlimited
power available to them, then the possibilities are
likewise unlimited. It must happen in and through
us - whatever happens to others. The responsibility
of the stewardship of this revelation is given to us
- but the resources available to, in and through us
are exceedingly greater than all our thinking and
asking.

IN THE CORPORATE BODY

A free rendering of the final verse in this chapter
would be "To him - the glory in the church and in
(or by) Christ Jesus to all the generations of the age

of the ages. Amen".

*One thing is sure, that it is God's purpose **NOW**, and in the eternal future, that in the Church should reside and be displayed "**THE GLORY OF GOD**". Can we be content with less than this?*

1. I therefore, the prisoner of the Lord, beseech you that ye walk worthy of the vocation wherewith ye are called,

2. With all lowliness and meekness, with longsuffering, forbearing one another in love;

3. Endeavouring to keep the unity of the Spirit in the bond of peace.

4. There is one body, and one Spirit, even as ye are called in one hope of your calling;

5. One Lord, one faith, one baptism,

6. One God and Father of all, who is above all, and through all, and in you all.

7. But unto every one of us is given grace according to the measure of the gift of Christ.

8. Wherefore he saith, When he ascended up on high, he led captivity captive, and gave gifts unto men.

9. (Now that he ascended, what is it but that he also descended first into the lower parts of the earth?

10. He that descended is the same also that ascended up far above all heavens, that he might fill all things.)

11. And he gave some, apostles; and some, prophets; and some, evangelists; and some, pastors and teachers;

12. For the perfecting of the saints, for the work of the ministry, for the edifying of the body of Christ:

13. Till we all come in the unity of the faith, and of the knowledge of the Son of God, unto a perfect man, unto the measure of the stature of the fulness of Christ:

14. That we henceforth be no more children, tossed to and fro, and carried about with every wind of doctrine, by the sleight of men, and cunning craftiness, whereby they lie in wait to deceive;

15. But speaking the truth in love, may grow up into him in all things, which is the head, even Christ:

16. From whom the whole body fitly joined together and compacted by that which every joint supplieth, according to the effectual working in the measure of every part, maketh increase of the body unto the edifying of itself in love.

PART 2

THE OUTWORKING OF GOD'S PURPOSE THROUGH THE CHURCH

CHAPTER 7

THE VISION FOR UNITY

(Ephesians 4:1-16)

1. VISION OF BODY ONENESS   (4:1-6)

   Vital Responsibility of the Body
   Spiritual Relationship of the Body
   Singular Uniqueness of the Body

2. VISION OF BODY GIFTS   (4:7-11)

   Gifts Function in Grace
   Gifts Proceed from the Ascension
   Gifts with Specified Responsibility

3. VISION OF BODY GROWTH   (4:12-16)

   Ministries in the Body
   Maturing of the Body
   Function of the Body

CHAPTER 7

THE VISION FOR UNITY

(Ephesians 4:1-16)

From this point on, we move into the second main part of the epistle in which we consider "The Outworking of God's Purpose Through the Church".

In the first three chapters of the epistle we looked at the "Unfolding of God's Purpose In the Church". There we saw the vision that the apostle Paul had of the Church as the Body of Christ, and of what it is called to be.

Here we are introduced to the vision that the apostle had of how the Church should function right now at ground level. It is not enough to see the vision of the Church as the Body of Christ simply as an ideal, realisable only in the glory land; something to be realised only after Christ returns to take His people to be with Himself for evermore.

The apostle Paul is exhorting everyone to get the vision clear, then to go on and walk in the light of it. In these first sixteen verses of chapter four of the epistle there is a clarifying of the vision; that God has made full provision for the fulfilling of this purpose in and through the whole corporate membership of the Body of Christ.

What is most important now, is that all see the responsibility that devolves upon every member of the Body. It must also be understood that this is not an onerous task where the saints are legalistically demanded to fulfil the impossible. This responsibility is borne in the light of all the blessings that belong to the members of the Body in the heavenlies in Christ; that the exceeding greatness of His power is available to those who believe: that the resources of grace and of love are provided for all who are involved. All can now behave willingly and joyously, delighting to do the Will of God and thus fulfil their holy calling with a sense of responsibility, awe and dignity that becomes and befits the members of the Body of Christ.

1 VISION OF BODY ONENESS (4:1-6)

VITAL RESPONSIBILITY OF THE BODY

"I therefore, the prisoner of the Lord, beseech you that ye walk worthy of the vocation wherewith ye are called".

When the apostle says "I therefore" he is throwing the believers back on the revelation already given. He means: 'in the light of the vision received, the unfolding of the purpose of God in the Church and the superabounding provision that He has made in His grace and power and love'. Every believer can now act with a sense of responsibility. There is no need for living our lives in the flesh with carnal-mindedness, with attitudes, motives and conduct that belong to the old nature.

The awareness of the grace, power and love available to the whole Church: in fact, the super-abounding ability of God, that operates in the saints to enable them to walk worthy of their calling, should inspire and bring them to a place of dedication and determination to walk in the light of the vision received as well as to believe with unfaltering faith for the fulfilment of the purpose of God in His Church at this time.

"I beseech you", the apostle Paul pleads. He is fully aware of all the tendencies in the believers to lose sight of the vision, to fall back into their old ways and to be inconsistent in their walk. Over and over, the apostle Paul in his epistles is beseeching or exhorting. The word for 'beseech' has the same Greek root as Comforter, which translates the word parakletos meaning 'Comforter', 'exhorter', 'enabler', 'encourager', 'strengthener'. There is an appeal, an encouragement, an exhortation in the apostle's heart as he writes this letter. He has been so captivated by the vision that it has called for the giving up of his whole life to its fulfilment. Thus should all the saints likewise be captivated and committed.

He describes himself as "the prisoner of the Lord". Compared to this, imprisonment in Rome or anywhere else is merely incidental. In the previous chapter of the epistle he appeals to the believers not to faint at his tribulations which were for them. There he describes himself as "the prisoner of Jesus Christ for you Gentiles". He was captivated by Jesus Christ. He was a bondslave of Jesus Christ. He was bound to Him as a slave to his master, willingly, lovingly, loyally. It was Jesus Christ Himself who had purchased him and redeemed him for Himself with His own blood. To the Corinthians he writes - "Ye are not your own, for ye are bought with a price". (1 Cor.6:19,20).

The apostle Paul was not appealing to the saints because he was a bondslave of a denomination, system, or organisation of man's instituting. He had met the Lord and had seen Him face to face. He understood clearly what the Lord Jesus Christ had done for him and realised that he had been redeemed by His precious blood. Once we understand, as the apostle Paul did, the reality of Christ and His finished work, not just for us as individuals but for the whole Church (for Christ loved the Church and gave Himself for it), to see as the apostle Paul saw and to know how Christ gave Himself so completely and fully for us, there will then be no desire or proneness to unfaithfulness in any of us.

The overcoming saints spoken of in Revelation "loved not their lives unto the death". (Rev.12:11). This was the spirit of the apostle Paul. This is what he meant by being a "prisoner of Jesus Christ". Being in prison in Caesarea, or in Rome, or anywhere else, was only incidental. It was Christ to whom he was committed and to Him that he was bound.

"To walk" - translated from the Greek, conveys the idea of walking about, meaning that in every detail of the believers' life their conduct should be worthy, consistent with the calling to which they have been called. This behaviour should be expressive of the dignity and honour of their vocation as members of the Body of Christ. They represent Him and reflect Him. They are His epistles - "known and read of all men".

106

Everyone in the Body should be aware of His calling, for God has spoken concerning each one. His call has already been given. The verb used here literally means 'were called', for it is in the aorist tense, which means that it is already done. It is already an accomplished fact. Every believer should be aware of the call of God in his life and that with the call comes responsibility. It is important to understand that God is working to a plan. It is His will and purpose that is being worked out. Thus, to realise that we, as the saints of God, have a part in His eternal plan, should be very humbling and sobering to us all. God is not haphazard or careless. He is purposeful and decisive.

The whole of this second part of the epistle is an appeal to the saints to act with a sense of responsibility, to behave with the dignity that becomes the saints of God, and to reflect the grace and glory of our Lord Jesus Christ in all of their living.

SPIRITUAL RELATIONSHIP OF THE BODY

"With all lowliness and meekness, with long-suffering, forbearing one another in love; Endeavouring to keep the unity of the Spirit in the bond of peace".

The dignity that characterises the believers is not that of conceitedness or carnal pride. This is the dignity of holiness and wholesomeness of life and living, causing us to walk with 'all lowliness, or humility of mind, or deportment'. That is why the apostle Paul appeals to the Philippians "Let this mind be in you, which was also in Christ Jesus: Who .... humbled himself, and became obedient unto death, even the death of the cross". (Phil.2:5-8).

The rest of verse 2 may be translated 'and forbearance with longsuffering, enduring patiently one another in love'. Again it is very evident that the major problem, even in the Church, is that of the relationship of one member with the other. This problem is, of course, common to mankind the world over, and in every age. In the vision received by the apostle Paul, however, the Body of Christ is seen to be different. He sees the whole Body as one, and "being rooted and grounded in love" the saints are enabled to relate to each other aright. This can only be done in the power and grace of the Spirit. The fruit of the Spirit is manifestly to do with members relating together in the Body. *(Gal.5).*

This is something about which we cannot be haphazard or irresponsible. We should always act with a sense of responsibility. We should continuously remind ourselves of the vision, keep close to Jesus and realise that we are bondslaves of Jesus Christ. We reflect Him. We are filled with His very life and His love - therefore, we can patiently endure one another. We can indeed be longsuffering in the power of the Holy Spirit, even when things are very trying and difficult.

This exhortation, to apply ourselves diligently, is apparent by the words *"endeavouring to keep the unity of the Spirit"*. This is not a man-made unity - a mere human attempt to **get things together**. *"By one Spirit are we all baptized into one body".* *(1 Cor.12:13).* It is the Holy Spirit Himself who makes the unity in His people. *"In the bond of peace"* means *'the binding together with each other in peace'.*

SINGULAR UNIQUENESS OF THE BODY

"There is one body, and one Spirit, even as ye are called in one hope of your calling: One Lord, one faith, one baptism, One God and Father of all, who is above all, and through all, and in you all".

The words *"There is"* are in italics in the King James version, because they are not in the original. They are only there to help us understand the meaning of the statement.

These seven unities here are clearly different aspects of this unity of the Spirit. We are exhorted - *"endeavour to keep the unity of the Spirit in the bond of peace .... one body, and one Spirit, etc."*

ONE BODY. This is the whole theme of the epistle and we have already seen that it is only the Holy Spirit Himself who can create the unity of the Body of Christ. Much of what happens in ecclesiastical life is carnal and the product of man's own thought. This is evidenced by the seeming insurmountable barriers that divide the Church. But the purpose that God has for His people, however, is *"one body"*.

Let us reflect on the exhortation to 'walk worthy of our calling'. The 'walk' spoken of is not simply our own personal concern for holiness of life and sanctified living, although that is obviously included, for in no other way would we be able to walk worthily of our calling.

The responsibility **here**, however, emphasises right relationships between each brother/sister in the Body of Christ. It is walking in the awareness of the oneness of the Body. God does not recognise our divisions, our labels or factions. These are just the products of carnal mindedness. (1 Cor.3). In this context, referring back to chapter 3 of the epistle, there is no way that we can walk like this except 'in love'. This is also further amplified in the words: "Forbearing one another in love".

ONE SPIRIT. Here we are introduced to the singular uniqueness of the Holy Spirit Himself. Again and again these two words 'One Spirit' are brought out in the ministry of the apostle Paul. Examples of this are seen in 1 Cor.12:4 "Now there are diversities of gifts, but the same Spirit"; 1 Cor.12:11 "But all these worketh that one and the selfsame Spirit"; 1 Cor.12:13 "For by one Spirit are we all baptized into one body"; and Eph.2:18 "For through him we both have access by one Spirit unto the Father".

In the midst of many heresies and the manifestation of spurious and strange phenomena, the apostle Paul is very quick to emphasise the uniqueness of the Holy Spirit Himself. There is no mixture nor opening of the door to strange spirits. In his ministry the apostle Paul had come across many situations where evil spirits sought to confuse situations.

For example, in Acts 16 the woman with the spirit of divination cried out all the right things - "These men are the servants of the most high God, which shew unto us the way of salvation". This was an attempt by the evil one to create the impression that the spirit which this woman had within her and the Holy Spirit which the apostles had, were one and the same spirit. The apostle Paul is emphatic about the oneness of the Holy Spirit - His singular uniqueness.

Also, the oneness of the Spirit in the Body is

utterly important, for, "he that is joined unto the Lord is one spirit". There is a oneness between the Holy Spirit and the spirit of each believer. When that oneness is clearly established, all the believers, who are sincerely joined to the Lord as one spirit, will inevitably find themselves flowing together in the unity of the Spirit. There cannot possibly be conflict between that which is of the Holy Spirit in one believer's life and another, whatever their label might be, or to whichever branch of the Christian church they each belong.

Once more, it is one Holy Spirit who is operating here, because only He can take the things of Christ and make them real to us. He alone can bring forth what is of the finished work of Christ and establish the Christ life in the believer. Only by the Holy Spirit can all the things, that are available to believers, become effective and real in their lives.

ONE HOPE. Actually, the words here mean 'even as you were called in one hope of your calling'. To understand the vision of this "one hope" helps us to grasp the importance of the exhortation for us to be "endeavouring to keep the unity of the Spirit in the bond of peace" - 'even as ye were called'. Is this not the hope of our calling, that the Body of Christ should be one body under His Headship, reflecting "the fulness of him that filleth all in all"? Is it not the hope of His calling that we should be the Church of Jesus Christ, manifesting "the manifold wisdom of God" to principalities and powers in the heavenlies? May God enlarge our vision, that we might see, in the wider context, the true nature of God's calling of His people - His 'called-out' ones, His ecclēsia. We need to understand the purpose for our being 'called out', as well as that for which He has called us.

ONE LORD. In 1 Cor.12:5 we have "And there are differences of administrations, but the same Lord". It is extremely important that all God's people confess and submit to the Lordship of Christ in a singular and decisive way. Many people give place to spurious, fleshly, devilish and even occult things, much of which is called religious experience. It is *little wonder that the apostle Paul says in 1 Cor.12:3, "No man can say that Jesus is the Lord, but by the Holy Ghost".*

When people speak of dominating things that overwhelm and subdue them; of the tremendous power of the devil over their lives; that such things hold lordship's sway over their lives, it is evident that there are areas not submitted to Christ.

All ground, exploited by strong, evil and spurious powers in people's lives, must be surrendered to Christ's Lordship, because Satan and his hosts will exploit such to the full. We must, exclusively, submit only to the Lordship of Christ. There is but one way in which the Lordship of Christ will manifest itself in all its fulness in the Church, - that is, when the Church is united together in the unity of the Spirit.

'Pentecostal' or 'charismatic' experience has been given to God's people so that the Lordship of Christ will be manifest in and through them. May God grant that we might see the unity of the Body of Christ in a fuller and more meaningful way than ever before, till there comes forth the revelation of the Lordship of Christ in the midst of the earth - through His people.

ONE FAITH. When we consider the multitudinous expressions concerning which we think the faith is about, we wonder how the Church could ever come to a oneness of faith. There are so many confessions of the faith, creeds, statements of fundamentals and tenets, varying from one branch of the Christian church to another, according to one system of theology or another. Surely the oneness of faith must mean something different from a mere written statement of beliefs.

Jude writes, "I .... exhort you that ye should earnestly contend for the faith which was once delivered unto the saints". (Jude 3). He qualifies this by saying, "For there are certain men .... turning the grace of our God into lasciviousness, and denying the only Lord God, and our Lord Jesus Christ". (Jude 1:4). It is clear from this, that the faith of which he speaks, centres in the person of our Lord Jesus Christ.

So it was with the apostle Paul in Gal.2:20 - "I am crucified with Christ: nevertheless I live; yet not I, but Christ liveth in me: and the life which I now live in the flesh I live by the faith of the Son of God, who loved me, and gave Himself for me". The new life in the believers is - **Christ's life**. It is Christ Himself wrought in us by the Holy Spirit, and the faith by which we live is His faith, the faith of the Son of God who loved us and gave Himself for us. "The faith" is literally - Christ Himself and His finished work.

Later in this chapter of Ephesians we will see that the purpose of the gifts of the ascended Christ to His Church is that they are given "till we all come in the unity of **the faith**, and of the knowledge of the Son of God, unto a perfect man, unto the measure of the stature of the fulness of Christ". The oneness of faith spoken of here must inevitably be the fulness of Christ manifest in "the Church, which is his body".

ONE BAPTISM. What can this mean when there are so many baptisms referred to in the Scriptures? There is a reference to the "doctrine of baptisms" in Hebrews 6:2. Jesus talked about the "baptism of suffering" in Luke 12:50. John's believers talked about a "baptism of repentance". In Acts 19 Paul ministered the "baptism in the Name of the Lord Jesus". Jesus talked about 'baptism of the Holy Spirit' in Acts 1:8. Paul talked about being "baptized into one body" in 1 Cor.12:13. What, then, is this "one baptism"?

We must see this in the light of the context, for only then can we know its meaning. The apostle Paul is talking about the unity of the Spirit, "endeavouring to keep the unity of the Spirit", which is the oneness of the Body of Christ. Therefore, this "one baptism" must of necessity mean 'that work of the Holy Spirit Himself who baptises us into one Body'. Whether this baptism takes place when we are baptised in water, or in some charismatic experience, or by the work of the Holy Spirit in regeneration, or in any other way, is not terribly important. What does matter is that we understand clearly that the only oneness the Body can know - is the oneness that is created by the Spirit of

God Himself. "By one Spirit are we all baptised into one body".

ONE GOD AND FATHER. This concept of the Fatherhood of God has gripped the apostle Paul, as we have mentioned more than once already. "One God and Father of all, who is above all, and through all, and in you all".

Surely this is not an arbitrary statement promoting a concept of the universal Fatherhood of God? Let us look at this context. He is talking about the Body - the unity of the Body. The burden of his heart is - that we should be united together, for there is only "one God and Father" of us all. He is over us all. It is His divine life that operates through us. It is His fulness that indwells the Body.

The Fatherhood of God is something unique, because the revelation of this came by Jesus Christ. It was He Himself who introduced us to the Fatherhood of God. Christ Himself is "the only begotten Son of God", but we are His sons by adoption through Jesus Christ our Lord. We have a father/child relationship together with God, and we have a brother/sister relationship in the family of God. We are one family. This family spirit, this family atmosphere is that which should pervade the whole Church of Jesus Christ. We are heirs together of God, and we are sharers together of the divine inheritance.

2 VISION OF BODY GIFTS (4:7-11)

GIFTS FUNCTION IN GRACE

"But unto every one of us is given grace according to the measure of the gift of Christ".

The verb for 'is given' is in the aorist tense and really means 'was given'. It is done. It is what is already provided for the Church in Christ. The noun for 'gift' also comes from the same root, so a fairly literal translation would read 'But to each one of us was given grace according to the measure of the gift of Christ'.

One thing is very clear, and that is that every member of the Church has already received the grace of God. (Of course many do not know this and so do not avail themselves of it). Every member here is seen as a gift to the Church, which is the Body of Christ. In the sense that each one is a gift, it means that, in no way, can any one be 'bought' by the Church. Each one is already bought by Christ and is given by Him to the Church. The Church can only receive such. Would it not be wonderful to begin looking at every member of the Church as a gift of Christ to the Body?

It is grace that has made each member what he or she is to the Body. It is by grace that everyone is saved. It is important that everyone understands this - that everything he or she is, is all of grace. We are, or have, nothing outside of grace. What we become by that grace, Christ Himself gifts to His Church. He has bought us all for Himself, that He might place us by grace as members in the Body, gifting us freely to His Body.

Later, we will see that there are some specialist gifts with specific ministries, but no one, whatever his calling, position or function, has anything to boast about. One's calling is wholly of the grace of God. **Everyone is a gift** to the Body of Christ, **a gift of the grace of God.**

To understand the meaning of this verse can be, for many people, a very liberating experience. So many people struggle to fulfil what they imagine is their calling, and they are uptight, tense, anxious, struggling, even trying hard and finding themselves frustrated in the effort. For me, it was gloriously liberating when I came to understand that I had been given grace according to the measure of the gift of Christ. I do not have to struggle to be what God has made me by His grace, or to be what He has empowered me to be.

We are nothing outside of His grace and can do nothing of eternal value. Clearly, while we all are gifts of Christ to the Church, the measure of the gift that we are will vary with each

114

individual. For some, the responsibility is much greater than for others. Some are fitted and called to greater degrees of responsibility in their steward-ship. But the grace given to each one is equal to the measure of the gift of Christ that that individual is in the Body.

This means that there is no need whatsoever for strain, tension, stress, worry, anxiety or for struggling. Whom God calls He equips. We must all learn to understand what our setting and calling is in the Body, and remember that grace has already been provided, to enable us to fulfil that calling and to function according to the gift of Christ, that we are in the Body. In this respect, the apostle Paul could say, "By the grace of God I am what I am: and his grace which was bestowed upon me was not in vain; but I laboured more abundantly than they all yet not I, but the grace of God which was with me". (1 Cor.15:10). Thus, the apostle Paul had nothing of which to boast, for both his standing and function in the Body of Christ were according to the grace bestowed upon him. In this way, we should all enter into the rest of faith and learn just to be ourselves. We need to understand that it is not our struggling or efforts, but the measure of grace imparted to us that fully enables us to function in our calling.

GIFTS PROCEED FROM THE ASCENSION

"Wherefore he saith ....". How enlightening is this. This adverbial conjunction - "Wherefore", simply means 'and for this reason', i.e. for the reason that every member to whom grace had been given is a gift of Christ to the Body. Concerning this, God had already spoken through the psalmist and prophet David and recorded for us in Psalm 68.

It has often been assumed that only those specialist gifts of verse 11 may be referred to as 'ascension gifts'. The apostle Paul's teaching here clears up this matter conclusively. Every member in the Body is a gift of Christ and, for this reason,

"He ascended up on high". ***All*** *are ascension gifts. It is now imperative for all the members of Christ's Church to lay hold of the vision for these days, and be rid of all the feelings of inadequacy, inferiority complexes and 'worms of the dust' concepts. These things are both irrelevant and false and hold the members of Christ's Body in utter bondage.*

It is also time now to clear up an important matter of truth, that is still often rather vague to the understanding of many of us. What does this mean: "When he ascended up on high, he led captivity captive"?

Generally speaking, it is acceptable to teach that rebellion, and all that makes for captivity: whether it be man's sin of disobedience, or satanic deception and pride, or the hostility of the hosts of darkness – all had to be overcome. In this sense, we can see what a mighty work of grace was wrought, when Christ came and descended into the lower parts of the earth through the incarnation and His death. Then, in His ascension above all the heavens, He led captivity captive and broke its power, all the fetters and chains of bondage were broken and the prisoners set free.

This, I believe, is perfectly true – but is not the whole of the truth. This portion may be interpreted as follows: 'Having ascended up on high He led captive a captive multitude'. This is perfectly in keeping with most Bible expositors and translators.

What then is this captive host or multitude? I now see this as referring primarily to the Church, for the following reasons:

1. *This statement is directly connected to verse 7, which wholly refers to every member in the Body and is quoted for this very reason.*

2. *In leading captive this captive multitude, it was with the express purpose of giving gifts to, or for, men.*

3. *This statement is a quotation from one of David's Messianic Psalms and in the Authorised Version is expressed as follows: "Thou hast ascended on high, Thou hast led captivity captive: Thou hast received gifts for men; yea, for the rebellious*

also that the Lord God might dwell among them". (Psalm 68:18). Therefore, the rebellious ones have been captivated by the ascended Christ and have themselves become the recipients of His marvellous grace.

4. The verb for "he led captive" is in the aorist tense, as are all the blessings spoken of concerning every member in the Body of Christ (e.g. Eph.1:3; 2:5,6). This means that what He accomplished in His ascension, is already an accomplished, finished work, wrought for all the saints. That, while He broke the power of Satan and sin for every believer, and dethroned the usurper (John 12:31), and took possession of the keys of hell and of death (Rev.1:18), the final chaining and judgment of Satan and his hosts is for a time still appointed. (Rev.20). This leading of captivity captive is already an accomplished fact - and must, of necessity, refer to the Church.

5. The whole concept of the Church being subject, not to evil powers any longer, but to Christ her Lord and that His Headship is over all things to the Church, His Body, is, throughout the whole epistle, connected with our Lord's finished work, culminating in "His mighty power, Which he wrought in Christ, when he raised him from the dead, and set him at his own right hand in the heavenly places". (Eph.1:19,20).

6. Finally, this glorious vision is in perfect keeping with the spirit of the apostle Paul, who made his plea and exhortation on the basis of his being "the prisoner of the Lord" (4:1), and "For this cause, I Paul, the prisoner of Jesus Christ for you Gentiles ...." (3:1).

He is declaring that he is literally a bondslave of Jesus Christ. He is captivated by Him, - he is one of that captive multitude, whom Jesus led forth in His triumphant ascension.

"Ye are not your own. For ye are bought with a price". (1 Cor.6:19,20). This means that, in His redemption, He bought us with His own blood out of captivity to Satan and sin's bondage, out of the condemnation of God's holy Law and its just demands and penalty, and that He purchased us to be *His* bondslaves for *Himself*.

What a glorious captivity — captivated by love, grace, truth, honour and the dignity of true manhood again; restored to dominion under His pre-eminent rule and authority to be our true selves; to be conformed to His image; to share in His eternal programme; to be part of His glorious Church, the revelation of Him "that filleth all in all".

Psalm 68 prophetically unfolds the divine purpose — "that the Lord God might dwell among them". Our text here declares that "He ascended up far above all heavens, that he might fill all things". Mankind will yet know that God dwells victoriously in reigning power amongst His people.

"We speak the wisdom of God in a mystery .... which God ordained before the world unto our glory: Which none of the princes of this world knew: for had they known it, they would not have crucified the Lord of glory". (1 Cor.2:7,8).

GIFTS WITH SPECIFIED RESPONSIBILITY

"And he gave some, apostles; and some, prophets; and some, evangelists; and some, pastors and teachers".

The word 'apostles' literally means 'sent ones'. Apostles are clearly called, commissioned and ordained by our Lord Jesus Christ and sent forth by Him, anointed by the Spirit of God, to fulfil the work of opening up peoples and nations to the gospel, establishing churches and the saints in the faith, exercising a spiritual wisdom and authority and reflecting the nature of Christ Himself, who has been described as the chief apostle.

The word 'prophets' shows clearly that their ministry was that of inspired utterance, foretelling and forthtelling the Word of God. The ministry, both of prophets and of prophecy, is primarily for edifying, exhorting and comforting the Church, the Body of Christ. (1 Cor.14). Often, prophets have revelation on the Word of Scripture, revealing insight into situations, confirming vital things and decisions, particularly of an apostolic nature. In fact, the apostle Paul says that revelation concerning the Church, which is the Body of Christ, has been given not just to himself, nor merely to the apostles, but to the apostles and prophets by the Spirit.

The word 'evangelists' means proclaimers or announcers of good tidings, or preachers of the gospel. As well as apostles and prophets functioning in the Body, there is a necessity for preachers of the gospel, who, also functioning in the Body, can present the gospel to the world. There is a sense in which every member of the Church is an announcer of good tidings. Apostles, prophets, evangelists, pastors and teachers should all be able to do an evangelistic ministry and share their faith with the people around them. Evangelists, however, are specifically called, set apart for this function, yet not independent, but interdependent, in their rightful setting and thus equipped for the proclaiming of good news to a benighted world.

The word 'pastors' literally means shepherds or herdsmen. Almost everywhere else in the New Testament this word is translated as shepherd. Examples of this are seen in Matt.9:36; 25:32; John 10:11,14,16, etc.

Every pastor should reflect Him, who is the true shepherd, the chief shepherd and bishop of our souls. Jesus saw the people as sheep without a shepherd and His heart was moved with compassion for them. He described Himself as the good shepherd who gives His life for the sheep. No shepherd is worthy of the name of Jesus unless he reflects the nature, character, grace and compassion of Him who is the chief shepherd.

Elders too, are referred to as having a shepherding ministry, e.g. Acts 20:28-30 and 1 Peter 5:2-4.

'Teachers' translates the word meaning simply teachers or masters. These fulfil a very important role in the Body of Christ. In fact, they are seen to fulfil an important function in the Body according to 1 Cor.12:28 – "And God hath set some in the church, first apostles, secondarily prophets, thirdly teachers".

It is quite significant, from Acts 13:1, that the company of responsible people gathered together at the new Christian centre in Antioch were "prophets and teachers".

There is a sense also, in which shepherds and teachers are often combined in the ministry, or a shepherd might equally have a teaching function.

3 VISION OF BODY GROWTH (4:12-16)

MINISTRIES IN THE BODY

"For the perfecting of the saints, for the work of the ministry, for the edifying of the body of Christ".

The way that this has been presented in the Authorised Version conveys the impression that it is purely the work of the specifically gifted ministers in the Body to fulfil all three tasks: i.e. the perfecting of the saints, the work of the ministry and the edifying of the Body of Christ. This had tended to produce varying forms of ecclesiasticism and has brought about an undue emphasis on what has come to be recognised as clergy and laity respectively.

In these days of spiritual renewal and further enlightenment about the ministry of the Body of Christ, it is becoming clearer than ever, that these gifted ministries in the Body are for the perfecting of the saints, so that the saints themselves should be brought to a place of maturity and completeness of character. The word "perfecting" literally means 'the completing of character' or 'making ready and fit for use'. Again the "work of the ministry" means 'the work of service, or of ministry'.

How important it is for every member in the Body to realise that he has been called to a function. Not one person in the Body should be considered as a non-functioning member. How can the whole Body be built up, if the responsibility for function wholly depends upon some kind of elite, ecclesiastical hierarchy, to the exclusion of the other members?

We have seen already, that to **everyone** has been given grace according to the measure of the gift of Christ. This is the enduement of the Spirit of God, who equips and enables **every member** in the Body to fulfil his or her function.

D.P.Williams (affectionately called Pastor Dan) early this century wrote: "The members have been set as it hath pleased Him. It is evident that **every member** has a part, in some way or another, in the Body. Paul, writing to the Ephesian Church, explains that divine government has been set in the Body for control, order and supervision, and to see that everything is carried on honourably, peaceably, **and to build up the saints for their ministry".** *

This man of God had been, to me and many of my generation during our teenage years, a real father in the faith. Through such men as he in those days came new light and understanding concerning God's order for the Church, His Body. At that time, it was very difficult for me to see and understand how this plan of God could be applicable to the whole Church of Christ everywhere, since most denominations had their own ecclesiastical structure, that did not seem to make room for such a plan to operate in a practical way.

Again, it was exceedingly difficult to see how this vision could be restored, when a major concept of church life centred primarily in the one man ministry. This man-made structure, in effect, called for a ministerial capability beyond what God had either purposed or intended for His Church. If apostles, prophets, evangelists, pastors and teachers were considered essential for the perfecting of the saints in this day and age, then our denominational systems would largely require that each of their ministers be the summation of all that is apostolic, prophetic, evangelistic, didactic and pastoral. This, however, could not possibly be, and as a result, the Church universally has tended to be unbalanced and deprived of vital ministries.

Some are apostles, but others are prophets, others are evangelists, others are shepherds and teachers. It is not possible that one man could be all of these. Because the Church has largely centred its ministry in one man, it has been deprived of many of the gifts

---

*
'Riches of Grace', vol.5, Nov.1929, No.2, p.50, Apostolic Church, Penygroes.

of the ascended Christ, that should have made possible the perfecting of the saints. Thus, our systems have, generally speaking, produced ministers fulfilling the role of pulpit supply and congregations composed primarily of pew-sitters. Surely this is not the purpose of God?

"For as we have many members in one body, and all members have not the same office (function): So we, being many, are one body in Christ, and every one members one of another. (Rom.12:4,5).

MATURING OF THE BODY

"Till we all come in the unity of the faith". The verb here means 'till we may arrive at the unity'. Therefore, when the apostle Paul was writing, he was aware that we had not arrived at this unity. There was a 'going on' to it. To-day in this move of the Spirit of God, this 'going on' to maturity is speeded up. The Holy Spirit has been given to us to make known these gifts of the ascended Christ to the Church, in order to bring the saints into this place of completeness in Him, where they can function freely and fully to the building up of the Body of Christ, so that we all may arrive at this place of the "unity of the faith".

What is the unity of the faith? For some, we may think this to be a particular set of doctrines, or what we may call fundamentals, or perhaps a statement of faith, or maybe a particular creed to which we subscribe. In verse 5 we already looked at this and have considered the meaning of "one faith". The rest of the verse clearly amplifies and confirms the meaning here.

If we imagine that we are going to arrive at a unity of the faith, expressed in uniformity of doctrine, or a statement of beliefs, to which every member of the Body of Christ is going to subscribe - surely this is unthinkable? This is not because anything is impossible with God, but rather because God is bigger than all our concepts or expressions of them. It may be exceedingly important, especially in these days of changing ·winds of doctrine, to subscribe to some sound fundamental, doctrinal statement. To imagine, however, that everyone should essentially subscribe to the same statement, may well merely limit God to man's thinking.

Surely the "unity of the faith" is consistent with "the knowledge of the Son of God" and 'for the body to grow to full manhood', "unto the measure of the stature of the fulness of Christ"? It is both individually and corporately **'knowing'** Christ as the Son of God. It is the Body experiencing and maturing in stature to His fulness. That is the 'unity of the faith'. Later we will see that, in "speaking the truth in love", we grow up, not into our systems of theology, whatever necessary place they may have in our church life; but "we grow up into him .... which is the head " - Christ.

The "knowledge" of the Son of God spoken of here means knowledge that comes from observing, perceiving and discerning Him. This was the kind of knowledge that transformed Isaiah's life. (Isa.6). This is the kind of knowledge Jesus prayed, to which His disciples would come. (John 17).

The word for 'man' here is 'andra' and is not the usual word 'anthrōpos'. The concept here is that of 'manhood'. And the word for 'perfect' means 'full grown or mature'. The maturity to which the Church has to come is described as "the measure of the stature of the fulness of Christ". We saw from chapter 1:23 that it is the Body of Christ that is "the fulness of him that filleth all in all". This is what the Church must be seen to come to, to arrive at, in its unity, in its togetherness, in its full function together. The building up is to that place where the Body expresses Christ in His fulness.

Verse 14 could be translated 'that no longer we may be infants being tossed to and fro (as by the waves of the sea) and being borne about (hither and thither) by every wind of teaching'. How like infants have believers often behaved through the centuries, in promoting our systems, divisions and carnality. We have literally contended earnestly for our particular bent of teaching, rather than having grown up into "the measure of the stature of the fulness of Christ".

The final word of this verse 14 is very revealing and challenging in the extreme - the word 'sleight' translates a word which is just like the word 'cube', from which the dice is made. The word for 'cunning craftiness' means 'craft or cunning'. Then we have the same word as in Ephesians 6:10, where it is translated 'wiles of the devil'. It means artifice or stratagem. The final two words in the Greek text mean 'error, or deceit'. Thus we have 'By the chance artifice (or stratagem or wile) of (error or) deceit'.

Every true believer who has come to a knowledge of the Son of God, will usually subscribe to the broad fundamental teaching concerning Christ Himself, His Person, His work, His Deity, His finished work, the efficacy of His blood, the reality of His risen life and ascension life. The tragedy is that ofttimes we major on the discrepancies and divergences that arise between one sect and another due to a difference in form of worship, and often merely incidental things about which God Himself is hardly concerned.

No true member of the Body of Christ will be weak on the basics of the Person and work of Christ Himself. Is it not then imperative that we cease majoring on many of these external, unnecessary differences and recognise that we share the fulness of His life together and that the law of the Holy Spirit in the Church is the law of life that is in Christ Jesus Himself?

If we do this, all this erroneous teaching and these carnal systems that minimise or detract from Him, the Son of the living God, will be exposed and rejected. We will be speaking and holding the truth in love and "grow up into him in all things, which is the head, even Christ". "For in him dwelleth all the fulness of the Godhead bodily. And ye are complete in him, which is the head of all principality and power". (Col.2:9,10).

FUNCTION OF THE BODY

How utterly important it is that all the Body grows to maturity, into Christ Himself. What a vital relationship the Body has to its Head, for verse 16 is impossible without this kind of relationship with Him. The very first word of verse 16 means 'out of', so it is having the right relationship with Him that enables the Body to function properly 'out of' or 'from' Him.

Only thus can His life pulsate through His Body.

The compound word meaning literally 'to join together fitly', and the compound word meaning literally 'to cause to unite together and be knit together', both have the preposition in front of them meaning 'together with'. Thus, the vision the apostle Paul had of the Church in its togetherness in chapter 3:6, is seen in practice here at ground level in the fellowship of the church in the community. Only as it is rightly co-ordinated, can the Body function properly. Every joint of supply is involved.

This is according to the working in the measure of each one part. In this way the increase of the Body and 'the building up of itself' in love is automatic. It just flows naturally from the togetherness, from the functioning according to the grace given, which grace is imparted "according to the measure of the gift of Christ". The word - poieitai - is middle voice and means that the increase is made of itself. Here is no struggle, no pressure, no tension - all function according to the grace imparted.

As we reflect on this chapter there remains one phrase that demands some emphasis: "en agapē", meaning - "in love". In verse 2 the members of the Body are exhorted to relate together - "in love". In verse 15 the conditions prevail for growing and maturing - "in love". In verse 16 the full function of all the members is exercised - "in love".

What binds all the members of the Body of Christ together in their fellowshipping, maturing and functioning is the love of Christ: that love which has been so beautifully portrayed in the third chapter of Ephesians.

> *"Bind us together Lord, bind us together,*
> *With cords that cannot be broken.*
> *Bind us together Lord,*
> *Bind us together with love".*

17. This I say therefore, and testify in the Lord, that ye henceforth walk not as other Gentiles walk, in the vanity of their mind,
18. Having the understanding darkened, being alienated from the life of God through the ignorance that is in them, because of the blindness of their heart:
19. Who being past feeling have given themselves over unto lasciviousness, to work all uncleanness with greediness.
20. But ye have not so learned Christ;
21. If so be that ye have heard Him, and have been taught by Him, as the truth is in Jesus:
22. That ye put off concerning the former conversation the old man, which is corrupt according to the deceitful lusts;
23. And be renewed in the spirit of your mind;
24. And that ye put on the new man, which after God is created in righteousness and true holiness.
25. Wherefore putting away lying, speak every man truth with his neighbour: for we are members one of another.
26. Be ye angry, and sin not: let not the sun go down upon your wrath:
27. Neither give place to the devil.
28. Let him that stole steal no more: but rather let him labour, working with his hands the thing which is good, that he may have to give to him that needeth.
29. let no corrupt communication proceed out of your mouth. but that which is good to the use of edifying, that it may minister grace unto the hearers.
30. And grieve not the Holy Spirit of God, whereby ye are sealed unto the day of redemption.
31. Let all bitterness, and wrath, and anger, and clamour, and evil speaking, be put away from you, with all malice:
32. And be ye kind one to another, tenderhearted, forgiving one another, even as God for Christ's sake hath forgiven you.

1. Be ye therefore followers of God, as dear children;
2. And walk in love, as Christ also hath loved us, and hath given himself for us an offering and a sacrifice to God for a sweetsmelling savour.
3. But fornication, and all uncleanness, or covetousness, let it not be once named among you, as becometh saints;
4. Neither filthiness, nor foolish talking, nor jesting, which are not convenient: but rather giving of thanks.
5. For this ye know, that no whoremonger, nor unclean person, nor covetous man, who is an idolater, hath any inheritance in the kingdom of Christ and of God.
6. Let no man deceive you with vain words: for because of these things cometh the wrath of God upon the children of disobedience.
7. Be not ye therefore partakers with them.
8. For ye were sometimes darkness, but now are ye light in the Lord: walk as children of light:
9. (For the fruit of the Spirit is in all goodness and righteousness and truth);
10. Proving what is acceptable unto the Lord.
11. And have no fellowship with the unfruitful works of darkness, but rather reprove them.
12. For it is a shame even to speak of those things which are done of them in secret.
13. But all things that are reproved are made manifest by the light: for whatsoever doth make manifest is light.

CHAPTER 8

WALKING IN THE LIGHT

(Ephesians 4:17–5:13)

1. LIGHT IN CONTRAST WITH DARKNESS   (4:17–24)

    Distinctive Walk of Believers
    Depraved Walk of Unbelievers
    Renewed Life of Believers

2. LIGHT IN CHRISTIAN FELLOWSHIP   (4:25–32)

    Honest in Conversation
    Controlled in Provocation
    Firm in Temptation
    Irreproachable in Trust
    Edifying in Communication
    Sensitive in Spirituality
    Ruthless in Discipline
    Charitable in Relationships

3. LIGHT IN COMMUNION WITH GOD   (5:1–13)

    The Sacrifice of Believers' Living
    The Sanctification of Believers' Living
    The Reproof of Believers' Living

CHAPTER 8

WALKING IN THE LIGHT

(Ephesians 4:17-5:13)

The apostle John declares: "God is light, and in him is no darkness at all. If we say that we have fellowship with him, and walk in darkness, we lie, and do not the truth: But if we walk in the light, as he is in the light, we have fellowship one with another, and the blood of Jesus Christ his Son cleanseth us from all sin". (1 John 1:5-7).

'Walking in the light' is also of the utmost importance to the apostle Paul. He declares, "We .... have renounced the hidden things of dishonesty, not walking in craftiness, nor handling the word of God deceitfully; but by manifestation of the truth commending ourselves to every man's conscience in the sight of God". (2 Cor.4:2). The whole of the portion now under our consideration deals with this sphere of the church's living, as a colony of heaven right here on earth. That sphere is 'the light of God'.

1 LIGHT IN CONTRAST WITH DARKNESS (4:17-24)

DISTINCTIVE WALK OF BELIEVERS

The force of the exhortation in verse 17 is that of a solemn appeal. This is made 'in the Lord', for it does not apply in the same way to those 'outside' of the Lord. Here is an appeal to those who are already committed to Him, and who have entered into the full provision of God's great salvation for His Church.

The word "therefore" takes us back to the context of the verse and means - it is 'in the light of the vision unfolded and of the responsibility that now devolves upon every member of the body', that this solemn appeal is made. It emphasises the distinctiveness of those who are members of Christ's Church. They are not their own. They live neither for themselves, nor to please men. They live their lives constantly in the light of God, for they are "bought with a price" and are captives for Christ.

Those who are members of Christ's Body are different from all other people. This does not provide a reason for pride, since it is what the grace of God has wrought in them. It is imperative, however, that that difference be seen. The believers need not be subject to the world's system of error and darkness. The appeal of the apostle Paul to the Romans is: "Be not conformed to this world", or as Phillips' translation portrays it: "Don't let the world around you squeeze you into its own mould". (Rom.12:2). How else will the world come to know about God, if they fail to see godliness in His people?

DEPRAVED WALK OF UNBELIEVERS

The nations are described as living "in the vanity", or 'religious error', "of their mind, Having the understanding darkened", or literally - 'having their understanding shrouded in darkness', "being alienated from the life of God through (on account of) the ignorance that is in them". The phrase, "the blindness of their heart", which ends this verse in the Greek text, means: 'the hardening or callousness and insensibility' of their heart.

Verse 19 describes what this insensibility has done to them. The words "past feeling" really mean 'to be in pain', or 'to grieve'. Literally, they have departed from the pain or grief of conviction, making them so insensitive to sin, that they proceed to live for themselves in intemperance and licentiousness. Thus, they freely perform or practice all uncleanness or lewdness and live so much for themselves, that they take advantage of others. What a description of the depravity of human life without God.

In retrospect, Ephesians 2:1-3 gives a parallel description of what life is like in the world, when people are alienated from the life of God. This was described as spiritual death, but the Church has come alive 'out from among the dead'. No more, therefore, should its members resort to the practices and behaviour of those who walk in darkness and exist in a state of death.

RENEWED LIFE OF BELIEVERS

"But ye have not so learned Christ; If so be that ye have heard Him, and have been taught by Him, as the truth is in Jesus".

How beautifully and significantly does everything here centre in the Lord Jesus Christ. It is He, Himself that we learn - all that is of Jesus Himself. That is why Jesus appealed: *"Take My yoke upon you, and learn of Me". (Matt.11:29).* In this way, it is Him whom we hear, and whoever the teacher may be, it is in Him that we are taught: for truth always centres in Jesus Christ Himself.

What have we learned of the truth that is in Jesus Christ, which affects us who are members of His Body? Verse 22 says *"That ye put off concerning the former conversation the old man"*. The words *"put off"*, being in the aorist tense and middle voice, indicate something which should already have been done - literally, *'for you to have put off from you the former mode of life, the old man'*. This is not something with which we are meant to battle continuously. We should have come to understand the completeness of the work, which has been wrought for us already in Christ. If there are continuing problems here, it will almost invariably be because we have not fully laid hold of Christ Himself and what He has accomplished for us.

The true ministry of the gospel centres wholly in Christ. It presents Him in His full and completed work. It declares and demonstrates that what He did was to take our place at Calvary. But more, for He also took our sin, weakness, frailty and impotence in the flesh and overcame all this for us, so that in and through Him, by the Spirit, we are now empowered to live and to walk worthy of bearing His precious Name.

This *"old man"* has been described as being morally depraved according to its desires, i.e. those things of deception upon which the heart has been set. We have put away these things and are finished with them.

This ability that believers have to *"put off ...."
the old man"*, is essentially related to verse 23 - *"And*

be renewed in the spirit of your mind". The concept of 'putting off' clearly refers to the 'fleshly' attitudes, motives and behaviour as the believers 'walk' in this dark world. Here, we are concerned primarily with the believers' relationships, both in the fellowship of God's people and in the world. The key to victorious living in these matters, lies in the 'renewal in the spirit of our mind'.

To be "renewed in the spirit of your mind" means 'the spirit which guides and rules your mind and which is now possessed and sanctified by the Spirit of God'. We have already seen from chapter 2 of this book how His Spirit relates to our spirit. It is by this spiritual relationship that our mind and heart are enlightened, renewed and disciplined. It is this kind of 'renewal' that enables us to enjoy the blessing of verse 24 - "And that ye put on the new man, which after God is created in righteousness and true holiness".

The force of 'putting on the new man' is similar to that of 'putting off .... the old man' in verse 22. This is something that we are considered to have done already. We have clothed ourselves with this "new man", which according to God was created spiritually, or invested with a spiritual frame in righteousness and holiness of truth.

Every true believer now lives - not after the old man, but after the new. His conduct is no longer in accordance with the old life, but rather with the renewed life, which is in Christ. He is alienated no more from the life of God, the understanding being shrouded in darkness, but he is walking in the light. The soul, with its emotions, affections, will, reason and thinking; the body, with its sense faculties, passions and desires: all now reveal this inward spiritual renewal and reflect the glory of the new life in Christ in all its manifest conduct and actions.

2 LIGHT IN CHRISTIAN FELLOWSHIP (4:25-32)

It almost seems a retrograde step, in that, having presented the vision of the glorious Body of Christ so clearly, with all the resources of grace, power and love available to its members the apostle Paul is suddenly having to deal with so many carnal and evil things.

This second part of the epistle, however, is concerned with the outworking of the purpose of God through the Church - the Church which resides here on earth. Being a colony of heaven on earth, the Church has to dwell, work and worship in a sickly, sinridden, devil-dominated world.

Why, then, should we imagine that *all* the members of the Church at Ephesus, or to whomsoever the apostle Paul wrote this letter, had reached such a stage of spiritual understanding and maturity, that the things, which we are now to consider, should not even have to be mentioned. Surely, He who said that He would build His Church did not mean that He would simply take a handful of people from the world and build **them** up in strength only. The upbuilding must also mean numerical upbuilding, for the Church is not a mere stagnant institution but it is ever progressing, ongoing, moving forward on the offensive, confronting the gates of hell and seeing them crumble before it.

With this kind of picture in mind, we see the Church alive, expanding, making constant inroads into the enemy's territory, seeing those, for whom captivity has already been taken captive, being introduced to the purpose of God for their lives. This is how it was meant to be and how it should be. In that case, the Church in the world needs all the vital and necessary instruction, particularly new converts, who ofttimes are simply feeling their way, and who, if bereft of compassionate understanding, may well feel overawed by the depth of spiritual maturity in the other members.

Thus, in this section, from verse 25 through to the end of the chapter, we have a series of instructions or commands, for most of the active words are given in the imperative mood. Clearly, it is vital that believers, especially those who are younger in the faith, be reminded of and instructed in these things. It must be remembered, however, that these commands have quite a different setting altogether from the giving of the Law by Moses. These instructions are given to remind us of what we, through grace and the Holy Spirit, are now enabled to do in every area of our lives. We are now able to live and relate to other people in honour and purity, in a world that continuously endeavours to impinge upon us with its fleshly and evil ways.

Believers are instructed to be -

HONEST IN CONVERSATION

"Wherefore putting away lying". This "putting away" means 'having put to death by renunciation or separation'. It is vital that new believers are given a clear, uncompromising start. Baptism, in the New Testament sense of the word, means 'being baptised into Jesus Christ's death' - i.e. death to self, sin and the old ways. (Rom.6). No believer should seek baptism who has not in his heart and mind that readiness and willingness to totally separate himself from all the falsehood and lying of the past. He now belongs to a new community, the family of God, in the Body of Christ. It is vital that he or she has a sense of responsibility in regard to relationships with all the other members, so that fellowship together and all conversation one with the other will be in openness, honesty and truth: literally, walking in the light.

CONTROLLED IN PROVOCATION

"Be ye angry, and sin not: let not the sun go down upon your wrath". "Wrath" here means: 'provocation to anger'. Clearly, there is a place for what one might call righteous indignation, or anger. Even the Lord Himself was angry with hypocrisy.

In relating one with the other, it is possible from time to time to be provoked to anger. At no time, however, should that anger lead to sin, or make us other than what the Lord would have us to be. To be angry, in the sense of sinning, would be to allow uncontrolled temper to rise; to have fleshly motives or attitudes in our anger; to be on the ego-defensive, regardless of what principles are at stake; to be partial with our dealings with people; not to be long-suffering and forbearing with weaker members of the faith, and so on.

In any case, neither the indignation, nor whatever

gives rise to it amongst the members of the Body, should be allowed to continue. The day should not even pass without the matter being settled. 'Let not the sun be setting upon your provocation'.

FIRM IN TEMPTATION

"Neither give place to the devil". This is one of the most vital instructions to the members of the Body. All sorts of things in the believers' lives can give ground to the evil one to exploit: e.g. compromising with sin; worldliness; involvement in fleshly attitudes, motives or conduct; submission to thoughts of fear, anxiety, unbelief, hardness or temptation, and such things. All these give ground upon which the enemy can take advantage.

Remember that Jesus said, "The prince of this world cometh, and hath nothing in me". (John 14:30). Throughout all His life and ministry, Jesus gave no ground to the evil one - not even for one moment of time. He was tempted, tried, assailed, persecuted, falsely accused and misunderstood, but He gave no place to the devil, and overcame him as a man in this very world. At the Cross He overcame him on behalf of every believer. For all who submit to Him as Lord, He has dethroned the usurper and has broken his evil power.

Therefore, it is unnecessary for any believer to give ground to the enemy. Jesus should be Lord in every area of one's life, and there should exist a right relationship between all the members in the Body. In this way the evil one will have no inroads to pursue or be able to impose his subtle strategy.

IRREPROACHABLE IN TRUST

"Let him that stole steal no more ...." How wonderful, that the ascended Christ "led captivity captive" in such a way, that sinners of every kind, even thieves and robbers, can have equal part in His Body with everyone else. But for such people life is now changed. Not only should there be a total trust-worthiness, but a going forward on positive ground "Working with his hands the thing which is good, that he may have to give to him that needeth". Such is the trust-worthiness of the saints of God, that not only are they now free from the reproach of such past corruption, but they are providing honourably for themselves, as well as for others less able and in need.

EDIFYING IN COMMUNICATION

"Let no corrupt communication proceed out of your mouth ...." Here is a command – not to allow any impure or foul word to proceed out of your mouths. This can, of course, relate to the past mode of speech, which may be blasphemous and unclean, yet when this is set against the rest of the instruction, we find that it has a fuller implication.

The kind of communication that proceeds out of believers' mouths should be that which is good for building up the members, positively giving grace to those who hear.

Conversely, anything that pulls down, destroys, undermines, divides; anything that sows seeds of doubt, discord or discontent; anything that is designed to destroy faith in others, or to give one's self an advantage before others: is corrupt. These things do not build up, nor impart grace. Let us be constantly reminded, that in our frequent opportunities to communicate, we ought to seek to edify and impart grace to the hearers.

SENSITIVE TO SPIRITUALITY

"And grieve not the Holy Spirit of God ...." True spirituality is the kind of life that the believer lives, where the Holy Spirit and the believer's spirit are one. "He that is joined unto the Lord is one spirit .... Therefore glorify God in your body, and in your spirit, which are God's". (1 Cor.6:17,20). The believer, who is inwardly renewed, will be very sensitive to that which is 'approved by', or 'aggrieving to' the Holy Spirit.

It is by the Holy Spirit alone that the believer is enabled to walk worthy of his calling. It is the Holy Spirit Himself who seals the believer "unto the day of redemption". We will remember from Eph.1:13, that the sealing with the Holy Spirit is 'that mark of distinction, that invests the believers with a certain character'.

This does not mean that the believer will be invariably faultless and perfect in every way. What it does mean is - that the moment sin enters and that which is displeasing to the Lord takes place, the Spirit-filled believer will immediately sense the jarring in the relationship between the Holy Spirit and himself. He will know that the Spirit of God is grieved, is vexed. He will want immediately to repent and confess his sin, thus to experience again the forgiveness and the cleansing of the blood of Christ. He will not, however, desire to return repeatedly to the same kind of thing. The word for grieve is in the continuous present tense and active voice and literally means, that the believer must not keep on doing wilfully, positively, consciously and deliberately those things that are grieving and vexing to the Holy Spirit.

RUTHLESS IN DISCIPLINE

"Let all bitterness .... be put away from you ...." This verse may well read, 'all bitterness and indignation and wrath and outcry (clamour, vociferation) and blasphemy (evil speaking, railing) let it finally and completely be seen to have been removed from you, together with all malice'. The words 'let it be removed' are in the passive voice and indicate that this can only be done by allowing the Holy Spirit to do it in us. "The law of the Spirit of life in Christ Jesus hath made me free from the law of sin and death". (Rom.8:2).

CHARITABLE IN RELATIONSHIPS

"And be ye kind one to another ...." This is what the Church is called to be like in its fellowship. It should be recognised that, with different members at varying stages of spiritual maturity, there is always the possibility of failure, weakness, or sin of some kind or other, overtaking one. In these circumstances, we are called to be "kind one to another", (gentle, benign, obliging), "tenderhearted" (compassionate), "forgiving one another". The measure of that forgiveness is exemplified in that which God has *extended towards us in Christ.*

This fellowship of God's people should be characterised in its binding together, by the very life and grace of our Lord Jesus Christ, that indwells the members by the Holy Spirit. There should never have to be the fear that any member has wilfully, deliberately gone out of his way to actively involve himself in sinful and compromising acts. That would be equal to tempting God. It is a command of the Lord that "Thou shalt not tempt the Lord thy God". (Matt.4:7). In the same way, the members of Christ's Body should not tempt one another. "Be ye kind one to another, tenderhearted, forgiving one another, even as God for Christ's sake hath forgiven you".

3 LIGHT IN COMMUNION WITH GOD (5:1-13)

THE SACRIFICE OF BELIEVERS' LIVING

"Be ye therefore followers of God, as dear children". The appeal to be "followers of God" is on the basis of being the family of God. The members of the Church are God's beloved, or "dear children". There should be a closeness of relationship that enables us to know God as Father and walk in the light of that relationship.

The word for "followers" means 'imitators' of God. We can only expect to copy whatever we see, and live in the light of what we know through the bond of loving relationship. This family relationship is a relationship of love. That is why in verse 2 we are introduced to the concept of 'walking in love, as Christ also hath loved us, and hath given himself for us, an offering and a sacrifice to God for a fragrant odour of a sweet smell'.

There is nothing so sweet and blessed as that of believers who bear this kind of fragrance: the fragrance of a life given up to God. The whole walk of the members of Christ's Body should reflect the nature of Christ in His sacrificial love, as He gave Himself for us. Let us remember also, that the offering and sacrifice of our lives is not first to men, but to God. We should be imitators of God, as His "dear children", walking in the simplicity and love of childlike faith and trust.

THE SANCTIFICATION OF BELIEVERS' LIVING

We may put verse 3 in the following words - 'But fornication and uncleanness (lewdness, impurity of motive) or all inordinate desire for riches or covetousness, let it not be once made mention of among you, according as is becoming the saints'.

In these days of permissiveness and licentiousness, the Church is called upon to maintain the standard of moral purity and dignity. We walk not to please men, but God, who is light. If believers are going to maintain trust-worthiness in fellowship, all their behaviour must be exposed to the light of God.

Verse 4 introduces us to what may well be a very sensitive area for some people. This verse may be translated as follows - "And filthiness (indecorum, indecency) and foolish talk, or jesting (buffoonery, ribaldry), which are not becoming, but rather thanksgiving'.

The entertaining and advertising media seem continuously to be promoting much that is corrupt in this area. Often, God's people subject themselves, sometimes deliberately, sometimes unconsciously, to the spirit of this age. There should be no involvement in things for which we cannot give thanks to God. The ability to give thanks to God should be the criterion of the rightness of our conversations.

God is not a killjoy, nor is He a God who has designed human beings to be so sanctimonious, that there is no room for humour. However, nothing that is unclean, or suggestive, or for which thanks cannot be given to God, should be heard or seen amongst the children of God.

Verses 5 and 6 clearly remind us that such things do not belong to the new life. They have no part in the kingdom of God and of Christ. Therefore, the believers are not to be deceived with such empty words. These are the things upon which the wrath of God descends in the sons of disobedience. The command is final and decisive. Do not be partakers together with them. In Romans, the apostle Paul makes his appeal, *"I beseech you therefore brethren, by the mercies of God, that ye present your bodies a living sacrifice, holy, acceptable unto God, which is your reasonable service", i.e. 'your spiritual or priestly service'. (Rom.12:1).*

THE REPROOF OF BELIEVERS' LIVING

"For ye were sometimes darkness, but now are ye light in the Lord: walk as children of light".

It is quite clear from this, that it is not what we say or do that is of paramount importance, but what we are. At one time, we were not simply *'in darkness'*, but we were *'darkness'* itself. Now, however, we are not merely *'in light'*, but *'we are light'* in the Lord.

Outside of the Lord, the unbelievers' lives are darkness and corruption, but in the Lord they are transparent, open, true, sincere. This *'being light'* affects all that believers do or say. Therefore, it is as *'children of light'* that we walk about now and live our lives, and the fruit of that light (or – of the spirit) is in all goodness and righteousness and truth. There is a purity and wholesomeness about this kind of life.

Since this new life is life *"in the Lord"*, which means that there is a vital relationship of the spirit of the believer with the Holy Spirit, i.e. they are joined together: then everything that the believer now does, is concerned with *"proving what is acceptable unto the Lord"*.

The word for *"proving"* has the same concept as Romans 12:2 – *"But be ye transformed by the renewing of your mind, that ye **may prove** what is that good, and acceptable, and perfect, will of God"*. In our text, it is in the present tense and active voice. This means that the believers go on applying themselves to that which is well pleasing to the Lord. Such is the nature of the relationship between the members of the Body and the Lord their Head, that mutual pleasure and delight are brought to the hearts of both. The good pleasure enjoyed by the Lord is also shared by His people.

The things of darkness are called *"unfruitful*

works". Contrast this with the fruit of light and note that this is in "all goodness and righteousness and truth". There is no fruit from darkness. What is done is a shame and it is dishonourable even to speak of it; those secret, undercover things. Believers are instructed to have no fellowship whatsoever with such, but instead to be discerning and reproving of them.

When the life of the believer is all light in the darkness of this world, and when he discerns and speaks words of reproof to the people, those words carry conviction and authority. What is said must spring forth from light, for it is the light itself that makes manifest the things of darkness. Verse 13 reads "But all things that are reproved are made manifest by the light: for whatsoever doth make manifest is light".

I am reminded in this section of what Jesus said about the Holy Spirit. He said, in giving promise of the coming of the Comforter, that "the world cannot receive, because it seeth him not, neither knoweth him". (John 14:17). Yet a little later Jesus said, "Nevertheless I tell you the truth; It is expedient for you that I go away: for if I go not away, the Comforter will not come unto you; but if I depart, I will send him unto you. And when he is come, he will reprove the world of sin, and of righteousness, and of judgment". (John 16:7,8).

Clearly, the Holy Spirit would not come to the world, but He would come to the believers, to the Church. It is the Holy Spirit Himself, filling, controlling and empowering the believers, in them and through them, who brings conviction to the world. Everywhere the Church and its members are, there should be a constant reproof and conviction of sin. Such should be the presence and power of the Holy Spirit indwelling the Church of God, that wherever her members are, there is a sense of godly fear pervading even the atmosphere.

The true Church of Jesus Christ is all light and makes manifest the unfruitful works of darkness. The light of God, indwelling His people, brings about a discerning and reproving of these unfruitful works.

14. Wherefore he saith, Awake thou that sleepest, and arise from the dead, and Christ shall give thee light.
15. See then that ye walk circumspectly, not as fools, but as wise.
16. Redeeming the time, because the days are evil.
17. Wherefore be ye not unwise, but understanding what the will of the Lord is.
18. And be not drunk with wine, wherein is excess; but be filled with the Spirit;
19. Speaking to yourselves in psalms and hymns and spiritual songs, singing and making melody in your heart to the Lord;
20. Giving thanks always for all things unto God and the Father in the name of our Lord Jesus Christ;
21. Submitting yourselves one to another in the fear of God.

CHAPTER 9

THE SPIRIT'S FULNESS

(Ephesians 5:14-21)

1. COMMANDS RELATING TO THE SPIRIT'S
   FULNESS   (5:14-18)

   > Awake and Arise
   > Live Wisely
   > Understand God's Will
   > Be filled with the Spirit

2. CONTRASTS BETWEEN DRUNKENNESS AND THE SPIRIT'S
   FULNESS   (5:18)

   > Self Control
   > Soundness of Mind
   > Freedom from Compulsion
   > Christ Centredness
   > Restored Dominion

3. CHURCH LIFE RESULTING FROM THE SPIRIT'S FULNESS
                                              (5:19-21)

   > Open Worship
   > Continuous Thanksgiving
   > Mutual Submission

CHAPTER 9

THE SPIRIT'S FULNESS

1   COMMANDS RELATING TO THE SPIRIT'S FULNESS

(5:14-18)

In verses 14 to 18 we have a series of commands, verbs that are written in the imperative mood, such as awake; arise; take heed; be not unwise; be not drunk; be filled.

AWAKE AND ARISE

This verse begins with "Wherefore he saith" and means 'for this reason God has already spoken'. The quotation that follows is usually accepted as referring to Isaiah 60:1 - "Arise, shine; for thy light is come, and the glory of the Lord is risen upon thee". In our text, the apostle Paul takes this and applies it to the Church.

The reason for this command, issued to the members of the Body, is that their fellowship with God and with each other is all 'in light'. "If we say that we have fellowship with him, and walk in darkness, we lie, and do not the truth: But if we walk in the light, as he is in the light, we have fellowship one with another ...." (1 John 1:6,7). The Church is commanded to be alive and risen from among the dead. There can be no fellowship between light and darkness; life and death; walking in the light and the works of darkness.

It is possible to have experienced divine life and the blessing of walking in the light, yet now to be found asleep, amongst those who are existing in a state of death and not alive to the things of God. The command to such is to awake. That word is in the present tense and means 'to come awake and stay awake'. The verb for 'arise' is in the aorist tense and makes a command meaning 'arise once and for all', never again to return to dwell among the dead. The promise to such is - "Christ shall give thee light".

It is Christ Himself, who is the light of God, who has come. The fulness of the Holy Spirit in the believer's life causes Christ Himself to shine out through them. It is His radiance that is manifested in them. This is the glory of the Lord that is "seen" upon His people.

LIVE WISELY

The Amplified Bible expresses it: "Look carefully then how you walk. Live purposefully and worthily and accurately, not as the unwise and witless, but as wise - sensible, intelligent people". No Christian should live or conduct himself like a fool. The way of the Holy Ghost is the way of wisdom and prudence.

"Making the very most of the time - buying up each opportunity - because the days are evil". (Amplified Bible). While there is a rest of faith to the people of God, the believer's life is one of commitment to Christ, of taking His yoke upon one and learning of Him, yet finding that His yoke is easy and His burden is light.

The Greek word for 'to redeem' translated means 'To buy out of the market', i.e. to buy back the time so easily lost by superfluous and irrelevant pursuits, slothful behaviour, worldliness and much else. There is a price to be paid. Jesus called it losing our life that we may find it (Matt.16:24,25). All our time and talents belong to God. These we had sold for nought but we now redeem them.

UNDERSTAND GOD'S WILL

"Wherefore be ye not unwise, but understanding what the will of the Lord is". This means that the believers should not be spiritually in the dark. If they are walking in the power of the Holy Spirit, they are walking in the light of God. This covers every aspect of their living and conduct.

The word for 'understanding' here, which has a prefix meaning 'together with', suggests a co-ordination of thought and understanding concerning everything in the believer's life. It is not sufficient to know the will of God for just certain areas of one's life. The will of God covers every aspect of one's life. If there is a lack of wisdom in one area it will affect the whole life.

A proper understanding of the will of God should enable the believers to walk wisely and in harmony with Him.

Both verbs in this command are in the present tense, which indicates that the command not to be unwise and the command to be understanding of the will of God should be heeded continuously. There should never be a time when believers are given to a lack of wisdom, or to moving outside of the will of God and going their own way, or the way that others demand.

It is utterly important that we all move in harmony with the will of God, because God is working to a plan. He has His own divine programme. He is not haphazard or arbitrary in the slightest degree. God Himself has ordained an eternal purpose in Christ Jesus our Lord. Since everything about the Church's life is 'in Christ', then all its affairs, its conduct, its attitudes and motives should be in harmony with that divine purpose.

This way of life is consistent only with being constantly filled with the Spirit. Those who walk in harmony with His will, enjoy His presence, His blessing, His peace. There will be constant joy and harmony in our walk with God in all the details of our life.

BE FILLED WITH THE SPIRIT

No true believer in the Lord Jesus Christ can evade a clear response to this urgent command, given not only to the saints at Ephesus, but to all the "faithful in Christ Jesus". Whatever the background, upbringing, denominational bias or doctrinal traditions, the call is urgent and imperative - "Be filled with the Spirit".

This is clearly a command, written in the imperative mood, and no believer can escape it. Many precious believers have long kept the door of their heart closed to what could be the most glorious and

blessed experience of their Christian life. To be filled
with the Spirit is the heritage of all who love the
Lord, yet because of unscriptural teaching on the one
hand and fanaticism on the other, many are afraid
to give heed to God's command.

All those who believe and teach that they received
the Holy Spirit when they were converted and that
there is now no more necessary experience, should
remember that this command is to believers, not to
the unconverted.

It is not unscriptural to teach the finished work
of Christ. To suggest, however, that that is wholly
accomplished in a believer at his new birth is
erroneous. If it were, all the scriptural teaching on
crucifying the flesh, growing in grace, walking in
the Spirit etc. would be irrelevant.

To teach that we received the Holy Spirit at the
new birth is not untrue - for we are born again of
the Spirit of God (John 3:6-8). But to teach that we
have received all that is possible of the Holy Spirit
is unscriptural. In that case, the command to
believers to "be filled with the Spirit", would be
completely unnecessary.

The particular emphasis of this command, however,
is seen in the tense of the verb. The word for "be
filled" is in the continuous present tense. It means
literally to '*BE BEING FILLED*'. It does not matter
to which theological persuasion we subscribe - this
is a command to **all** believers.

The implication is that there is no once-for-all
experience of being filled with the Holy Spirit. The
believer's walk should be such that he is in that
place of communion with God and dedication to His
will, that he is constantly being filled with the
Spirit. This becomes most evident as we examine the
characteristic features of the Spirit-filled life, some
of which we have already noted in the context.

2   CONTRASTS BETWEEN DRUNKENNESS AND THE SPIRIT'S FULNESS   (5:18)

A closer look at the text brings out the following

meaning: *'Be not drunk with wine, in which is dissoluteness (laxity in morals, indiscipline, debauchery) but be being filled with the Spirit'.*

It is quite evident that many people are afraid to respond to this command. Reactions of fear and even antagonism have sometimes resulted from unsound and unscriptural practices, that have been considered as being of a pentecostal nature. Even spurious and strange mystical phenomena are sometimes said to result from being filled with the Spirit.

Those who excuse their excesses, on account of *'being drunk with new wine'*, should look again into the Word of God. Some may say: *'What about the day of Pentecost, when there came that breath from heaven filling all the house where the believers were sitting and cloven tongues like as of fire sat upon each of them and all were filled with the Holy Ghost and spoke in tongues as the Spirit gave them utterance?'* Of them it was said: *"These men are full of new wine ...."* (Acts 2:13).

That day the apostle Peter stood up in the midst of them all and said, *"....these are not drunken, as ye suppose .... this is that which was spoken by the prophet Joel; And it shall come to pass in the last days, saith God, I will pour out of my Spirit upon all flesh ...."* (Acts 2:15-18).

One thing most abundantly clear is that on the day of Pentecost, the drunkenness, of which the believers were mockingly accused, had none of the characteristic features of alcoholic intoxication, save the evidence of power, ecstasy and joy. To reflect on the record of those early days of Pentecost reveals what glorious times they were.

Men said: *"These men are full of new wine"*. Peter said: *"These are not drunken as ye suppose"*. They were inspired, empowered, revived and refreshed. They spoke in other tongues the wonderful works of God. The lives of all the believers and of the apostles were dramatically transformed. The living God was moving and speaking. Christ was exalted and magnified in the midst of that vast congregation.

There was nothing of a chaotic nature nor of confusion whatsoever. Even Peter, until then so excitable, so impulsive, so weak, so afraid - stood before his would-be persecutors in full command of himself and of the situation before him. He stood erect, unafraid, boldly and courageously, fired with holy zeal and empowered by the Spirit of God. He spoke with conviction and Divine authority. Multitudes were pricked in their hearts and convinced of the reality of the living Christ. Three thousand souls found Jesus Christ as Saviour and Lord.

What a day. Glorious day. Confusion? Disorder? Excess? **NEVER.** What unity and harmony, what blessing and power, what faith, love, joy and peace. Christ, crucified but fifty days or so before, was now seen to be Christ glorified, along with indisputable evidence that He was Lord - not only in the Glory, but right there in the midst of the people - by the Holy Ghost.

As we closely examine the teaching of God's Word, we will find no ground whatsoever for fear. In fact, the apostle Paul is quick to remind Timothy that "God hath not given us the spirit of fear; but of power, and of love, and of a sound mind". (2 Tim.1:7).

In the days of Pentecost the believers had "all things common .... and great grace was upon them all". (Acts 4:32,33). Beautiful day, wholesome and blessed in every way such as never had been before. When it is the Holy Ghost, there is nothing spurious or of a dubious nature, or anything that will produce fear, or tend to drive us from the Lord. What is of the Spirit of God is most lovely and a beautiful thing to behold. Christ becomes so real and men know that He is alive to-day and that He is Lord - "the same yesterday, and to-day, and for ever". All true charismatic experience will portray in those thus blessed all the evidences of the Grace of God.

It is clear from the text, however, that there is some kind of relationship between being "drunk with wine, wherein is excess" and being "filled with the Spirit". While the issue is clear - "Be not drunk with wine", it is, at the same time, most important that we understand why he relates the two things at all. Failure to have this clarified has often led to mis-understanding and even erroneous practices, sometimes by sincere, well-meaning people. It is absolutely essential to understand the relationship between these two things.

It is always necessary to rightly divide the Word of God, and that is no less true in this instance. This text must not be isolated from the passage from which it is taken. The context has a vital bearing on it, and it upon the context. In this sense, as we have seen already, it is most evident that the relationship spoken of is not one of **COMPARISON**: it is rather one of **CONTRAST**.

The Amplified Bible translates it - "And do not get drunk with wine, for that is debauchery; but ever be filled and stimulated with the Holy Spirit". Is it not unthinkable to compare any anointing, infilling or ministry of the Holy Spirit with debauchery? In the things of God there is only one Spirit - the Holy Spirit. 'Holy Spirit' in Welsh is YSBRYD GLAN and means the 'Clean Spirit', the 'Pure Spirit'. How dare we link any debauchery or excess in any form with Him.

The Holy Spirit is no mere influence, He has personality. He is none less than God Himself in all the perfection, beauty and loveliness of His nature. Every ministry of the Holy Spirit is characterised by Holiness. We do not need to be afraid of Holiness. He has not come to judge and condemn us if we are believers, but rather, to reveal to us Him who has taken our judgment and condemnation. Thus, with the Holiness comes the love of God in Christ Jesus our Lord.

What a time we are now living in. These are days of strife and calamity, nationally and internationally. These are days of growing apostasy and powerless formalism in much of our organised church systems, and all around, people and nations are utterly morally, spiritually and economically bankrupt. But to those who are "children of light" and who do not walk in darkness and who are in the know of the things of the Spirit of God, these are **WONDERFUL DAYS**.

These are days when God says He will cause to come down for us "the rain, the former rain, and the latter rain in the first month". (Joel 2:23). This is the day of restoration, the day of the moving of the Spirit of God, and we do not need to be afraid.

It was not so long ago, when to speak of a scriptural Pentecostal Holy Ghost experience would, in many branches of the Christian Church, have been greeted with horror and opposition, to say the least of it. Now, however, the wind of change is blowing, and as on the day of Pentecost the sound is coming from heaven.

There is no need whatsoever for any sincere Christian believer to fear the things of the Spirit of God. There is no need to be afraid of the Spirit of God. Everything about the Holy Ghost is divine, wholesome, lovely and beautiful. All fear should be put to flight and instead we should enjoy the freedom and confidence of living faith. The God who at Pentecost moved so wonderfully, powerfully and gloriously, bringing forth Christ in Glory and Power into the midst of the early Church, is doing the very same to-day.

Let us now examine some of these contrasts between drunkenness and the Spirit-filled life:

SELF CONTROL

A drunken man has no self-control, self-restraint or moderation in anything. But the Spirit-filled believer has complete self-control and moderation, for indeed this is a fruit of the Spirit. "But the fruit of the Spirit is love, joy, peace, longsuffering, gentleness, goodness, faith, meekness, **temperance**". (Gal.5:22,23). 'Temperance' is the old English word for 'self-control'.

Those who are frightened of the infilling of the Spirit of God, because of the uncertainty as to what will happen, and the possibility that they may lose control, need not fear. Look at any example of the Spirit-filled apostles in the early Church. They have full control of themselves and are in complete command in the Name of the Lord, of whatever happens before men or the powers of darkness.

God made us in His image and likeness. This image was marred by sin, but is restored to believers in Christ. Thus God has made us responsible beings, fully capable by His grace of controlling ourselves. Even when the gifts of the Spirit are bestowed upon the believer, their operation comes under one's full control. 1 Corinthians 14 was written partly to reveal this truth, so that all things are done decently and in order and the Church edified.

SOUNDNESS OF MIND

"God hath not given us the spirit of fear; but of power, and of love, and of a sound mind". (2 Tim.1:7) The Greek word for 'sound mind' means more than just 'self-control'.

This, indeed, is the very opposite to the drunken state, for in that condition one relinquishes sober and balanced mental responsibility. This is not so with the Spirit-filled believer. God calls upon him to reason. He quickens the memory and He **commands** the believer not to yield his life to Him by an abandoned passive submission, but rather by intelligent active co-operation with Him. (Rom.6:13).

Anything less than soundness of mind is not of the Spirit of God. What is of the Spirit of God does not produce an unbalanced mind, loss of control, or loss of power to think, will, act and to co-operate actively with God. God's will for the believer is - to be filled with the Spirit and to have soundness of mind.

FREEDOM FROM COMPULSION

A drunken man, having lost control and unable to think clearly, is under an evil influence and is driven. When the Holy Spirit comes in, He does not drive or force - He leads. "For as many as are led by the Spirit of God, they are the sons of God". (Rom.8:14). It is the Holy Spirit who leads, but the believer who chooses to follow. He is in full command of himself and all his faculties. When the Holy Spirit fills the believer, He does not take the place of the believer's spirit, for "The Spirit itself beareth witness with OUR spirit, that we are the children of God". (Rom.8:16).

CHRIST CENTREDNESS

The Spirit-filled believer never seeks to draw attention to himself. This is just what a drunken man does. The Spirit-filled believer, in contrast, seeks to draw attention to his glorious Saviour and Lord. Jesus said that the Holy Spirit would testify of Him. (John 15:26). "He shall not speak of himself .... He shall glorify me: for he shall receive of mine, and shall shew it unto you". (John 16:13,14).

RESTORED DOMINION

Drink, drugs, fleshly passions, Satan and demons, witchcraft, spiritism etc. all dominate men's lives. God's purpose for man was to have dominion (Gen.1:28; Psalm 8:6), but he abdicated that responsibility and submitted it to the serpent. (Gen.3:14-19).

The dominion, lost to mankind in the Fall, has been restored to every believer in Christ. They **"REIGN IN LIFE** by one, Jesus Christ".** (Rom.5:17;Rev.1:5,6; Rev.5:9,10).

3   CHURCH LIFE RESULTING FROM THE
SPIRIT'S FULNESS   (5:19-21)

What now follows is wholly dependent upon the members of the Body living their lives in the constant fulness of the Holy Spirit. The gathering together of God's people for worship and the commitment of each member the one to the other in terms of genuine spiritual fellowship, are exceedingly vital, if the believers are going to maintain the spiritual glow in a world of darkness like this.

These next three verses give a description of what the Church is meant to be like in its fellowship and worship. Only as each member is anointed with the Spirit of God can it be like this. Living in this world, having to cope sometimes with upsetting domestic situations, being often affected by challenging, emotive circumstances: all this could, without the Spirit, create emotional instability, making it almost impossible for the Church to function in this free, flowing way. Life in the Spirit, however, enables the members to live with thanksgiving above all these things and to be a revelation to this world of the glory of God - for this is the divine provision - "And the glory of the

Lord is risen upon thee".

OPEN WORSHIP

This word "speaking" is in the continuous present tense and in the active voice, as are all such words in this portion, e.g. singing and praising, giving thanks, submitting. This means that such acts of worship and commitment in fellowship are the natural outflow of the fulness of the Spirit, experienced by the people of God. There is nothing forced, nor anything especially planned. It is rather like what Jesus promised to those who thirst, that "Out from (their) innermost beings springs and rivers of living water shall flow (continuously)". (Amplified Bible John 7:38).

When God's people come together, filled with His Spirit to worship, there is a speaking out to one another of "psalms and hymns and spiritual songs". "Spiritual songs" here clearly indicate something different from "psalms and hymns". This is what the apostle Paul had spoken about in 1 Corinthians 14:15 "I will pray with the spirit, and I will pray with the understanding also: I will sing with the spirit, and I will sing with the understanding also". Clearly, the context there is in connection with speaking or singing with other tongues. Here in Ephesians it is the same. "Spiritual songs" are songs of the Spirit. Churches and fellowships have largely lost the art of singing spiritual songs. Spiritual songs in the Church are quite in order, provided that there is unity and harmony. When the apostle wrote of this in Corinthians, he was thinking of his own personal worship; singing in a personal way to God. But from our text, it is quite right and edifying for us to speak out to one another in spiritual songs.

When we praise God in the Church, there should be due regard for one another. There should not be unruliness or indecorum. When we worship thus, we are speaking to God, and there is a sense in which the Church is being edified, or built up in its worship.

Thus, in the worship from God's people, there should be manifest a combining of all, in glorious, *united and harmonious spiritual song. There should not be the problem of particular individuals asserting themselves, or drawing attention to themselves. When believers are continuously being filled with the Spirit, there will be a spontaneity about uniting in spiritual worship. Thus will all the attention be concentrated on Christ Jesus the Lord, for it is the Holy Spirit's objective and ministry to glorify Christ.*

"It came even to pass, as the trumpeters and singers were as one, to make one sound to be heard in praising and thanking the Lord .... then the house was filled with a cloud .... for the glory of the Lord had filled the house of God". (2 Chron.5:13,14). If that was the purpose of God for His people at the dedication of the Temple made with hands, what of the New Testament Church, which is being built of living stones - "for an habitation of God through the Spirit". (Eph.2:22).

It should not be surprising, therefore, if the members of the emerging Church, the Body of Christ, charismatically endued, are found singing and praising with their hearts to the Lord.

CONTINUOUS THANKSGIVING

"Giving thanks always for all things ...." The preposition *"for"*, when used with the genitive case (as here) means 'over' or 'above'. Thus, whatever happens to the believers as they live the Spirit-filled life, over and above all these things, seemingly good or bad, they will be giving thanks at all times.

Such thanksgiving is addressed to God the Father, in the Name of our Lord Jesus Christ, through whom we have been brought into this beautiful family relationship. To be able to continuously give thanks is one of the most precious evidences of intimate and vital relationship between the Father and His children. It indicates the reality of living faith in those thus exercised.

MUTUAL SUBMISSION

"Submitting yourselves one to another in the fear of God". This is a feature of Christian fellowship that has been either overlooked, or misunderstood, and

sometimes even misapplied.

At last, this important subject of submission to one another in the fear of God has been restored. The principle of submission is very scriptural and, if fulfilled in the right spirit, becomes the basis of meaningful fellowship with all the sharing, caring and covering that it provides for all the Lord's people. *

---

* This is a vital, yet implicating subject. Certain elements of teaching propagated in relatively recent times, have, when applied in an unscriptural or carnal way, tended to produce imbalance, division in the Body, and sometimes serious hurt. Notes have been prepared on the subject of "Submission and Authority" and these may be obtained by applying to the address inside the cover.

22. Wives, submit yourselves unto your own husbands, as unto the Lord.

23. For the husband is the head of the wife, even as Christ is the head of the church: and he is the saviour of the body.

24. Therefore as the church is subject unto Christ, so let the wives be to their own husbands in every thing.

25. Husbands, love your wives, even as Christ also loved the church, and gave himself for it;

26. That he might sanctify and cleanse it with the washing of water by the word,

27. That he might present it to himself a glorious church, not having spot, or wrinkle, or any such thing; but that it should be holy and without blemish.

28. So ought men to love their wives as their own bodies. He that loveth his wife loveth himself.

29. For no man ever yet hated his own flesh; but nourisheth and cherisheth it, even as the Lord the church:

30. For we are members of his body, of his flesh, and of his bones.

31. For this cause shall a man leave his father and mother, and shall be joined unto his wife, and they two shall be one flesh.

32. This is a great mystery: but I speak concerning Christ and the church.

33. Nevertheless let every one of you in particular so love his wife even as himself; and the wife see that she reverence her husband.

CHAPTER 10

MARRIAGE IN THE LORD

(Ephesians 5:22–33)

1. THE RELATIONSHIP OF LOVE   (5:22–24)

    Maturity of Husbands
    Submissiveness of Wives
    Accountability of Headship
    Submission to Christ's Headship

2. THE SACRIFICE OF LOVE   (5:25)

    The True Nature of Headship
    The Example of Christ's Headship

3. THE GLORY OF LOVE   (5:26–30)

    The Glory of Christ reflected in His Church
    The Glory of the Husband reflected in his Wife

4. THE BOND OF LOVE   (5:31–33)

    Marriage – Divinely Ordained
    Marriage – Mystery of Christ and His Church

CHAPTER 10

MARRIAGE IN THE LORD

(Ephesians 5:22-33)

The apostle *Paul* in verse *32* declares - *"This is a great mystery: but I speak concerning Christ and the church"*. In this portion we are examining one of the most beautiful aspects of the purpose of God in human life. For many people, the wording used in this portion sometimes creates considerable emotive response. There are two main reasons for this: First, there is a lack of understanding concerning the teaching here; secondly, there is a lack of appreciation of the fact that God has purposed the very best for His people.

As we reflect and consider what is going on in society around us and in the world in general in our generation, there is much cause for grief, as we behold the tragedy of broken marriages and divided homes. So much of what is happening brings sorrow to our hearts. When, on the other hand, we consider the purpose of God in Christian marriage and we see the outworking of that in their marriage and home life, we have much cause to give thanks to God. There we see love, security, stability; true love as God intended it should be.

1   THE RELATIONSHIP OF LOVE   (5:22-24)

As we now approach this study, let us put aside all preconceived ideas, all misunderstanding, feelings of antagonism and with an unbiased heart and mind look faithfully at our text. We will find that, right at the heart of all the teaching, here is Christian love at its highest and best. Outside of this, marriage has no real meaning.

MATURITY OF HUSBANDS

"Wives, submit yourselves unto your own husbands, as unto the Lord". It is very important that we understand the kind of men these husbands are meant to be. The word for *"husbands"* really means *'men with the dignity and authority of true manhood'*; men of spiritual and moral stature and maturity.

Unless this is understood, in our zeal to try and conform in all things to the commands of the Word of God, we may find ourselves subjecting wives to some of the most unwholesome and intolerable conditions. That, surely, was never God's intention. If wives are commanded to submit to their own husbands *"as unto the Lord"*, then this may only be possible to the extent that their husbands reflect the Lord in their lives and character.

It is quite impossible for wives to submit to their husbands *"as unto the Lord"*, if these men behave like devils. In no way is there a suggestion of unconditional or unquestioning submission. Wives are not commanded to subject themselves to dictatorialism, domination or tyranny. True Christian marriage depends very much on husbands who have a due sense of responsibility concerning their role.

SUBMISSIVENESS OF WIVES

This is a command to Christian wives to submit themselves to their own husbands. The word for *"submit"* is in the continuous present tense and means *'be submitting yourselves'*. Some people have expressed antagonism to the apostle Paul for this, as though he were something of a woman oppressor. He was not alone, however, in this kind of instruction. The apostle Peter also commands, *"Likewise, ye wives, be in subjection to your own husbands .... For after this manner in the old time the holy women also, who trusted in God, adorned themselves, being in subjection unto their own husbands".* (1 Peter 3:1,5).

After man's Fall in the garden of Eden: *"Unto the woman he said .... thy desire shall be to thy husband, and he shall rule over thee"* (Gen.3:16). Why did God ordain such a place for women? Many have conveyed the idea that God shows in this, respect of persons and makes the woman unequal to the man. This however, is neither an issue of inequality, nor of partiality.

ACCOUNTABILITY OF HEADSHIP

"For the husband is the head of the wife, even as Christ is the Head of the Church".
God is a God of order. In all societies there must be an authority that can govern, keep order, bear responsibility, interpret what is lawful and so on. There must be a governing authority responsible for defence, security and protection. Leadership for guidance and control in all the affairs relating to society is utterly essential. Similarly, both in marriage and in the Church, God has established Headship. *"But I would have you know, that the head of every man is Christ; and the head of the woman is the man; and the head of Christ is God". (1Cor.11:3).*

To understand both the nature and function of that Headship is exceedingly important. Not to understand, or to have a wrong understanding, will either cause people to be afraid of the subject and thus to ignore it, or perhaps arouse rebelliousness. In fact, this is such an age of rebellion against any form of authority, that we have the rise of anarchy in society. In the Church this brings chaos, and in marriage dissolution.

The custom and symbolism of head-covering, taught by the apostle Paul in 1 Corinthians 11:1-16, is primarily concerned with Headship. Christ the Messiah's Headship was God Himself - His covering. Hence you see *Him constantly in communion with His Father, having come not to do His own will, but the will of Him that sent Him".* He submitted all His plans, His work, His words to His Father, so that He could clearly say that all His works and words were not His own but His Father's. Jesus was in total submission to His Father's will. *(John 14:10; 4:34).*

The Head of every man is Christ. The man, who is not submitted to Christ as His Lord and subject to His Headship, is without a God-ordained covering. Instead, he may thus be subject to the intrigue and whims of men, or perhaps exposed to the subtle

162

deceptive stratagems of Satan and his hosts.

To be subject to Christ means that we have the covering of One who is Lord of all, who has dealt with every area of mankind's complex problems and delved into all the unholy operations of satanic principalities and powers. Everything has been put under His feet. He reigns supreme. He is Lord of all. All power and all authority in Heaven and in earth are in His hands. To become subject to Him means that we have the covering of the One in whose hands is all authority, universally.

What about women then? Cannot a woman submit herself to Christ direct, without having to subject herself to any man? Is it not true that "There is neither Jew nor Greek, there is neither bond nor free, there is neither male nor female: for ye are all one in Christ Jesus? (Gal.3:28).

It is very evident from all the Scriptures, that women have equally as important a place in God's care and love as men. There is not the slightest hint of women being unequal, or second-class, or being incapable of controlling their own affairs. Throughout the Bible women are given ample place and scope. It is upon both men and women that the Spirit of God is being poured according to the promise of Joel and confirmed by Peter in Acts 2. Both men and women are given the gifts of the Spirit and are called of God to function in prayer and prophecy in the Church. There is not the slightest hint in the Word of God of any man, other than the Man Christ Jesus being the mediator between women and God, any more than there is for men.

Women laboured with the apostle Paul in the Gospel. (Phil.4:3). Philip the evangelist had four daughters who prophesied. (Acts 21:8,9). Both Aquila and Priscilla taught and expounded to Apollos, the apostle, "the way of God more perfectly". (Acts 18:24-26). Both Aquila and Priscilla are quoted by the apostle Paul as his helpers in Christ Jesus. (Rom.16:3). Phoebe is referred to as a deaconess of the church and the saints are asked to assist her in all her business and service. (Rom.16:1,2).

It is important, therefore, that we understand the nature and function of Headship. God has not ordained woman for the role of headship. That role He has given to man. God has ordained women for other functions, but not the function of headship. And just as Christ was submitted to the Headship of His Father, and man is submitted to the Headship of Christ, so the head of the woman is the man. (1 Cor.11:3).

Of course, submission in marriage is not totally one way. Each submits to the other in sharing their problems, in discussing marital affairs, desires and purpose, and even assisting each other in arriving at decisions. There is total openness, trust, care, understanding and discipline. All the things that we have described in the principles of submission one to another, apply to the marriage bond.* In His God-given role of headship, however, the man is held accountable to God. He it is who bears responsibility for the affairs of his marriage and family.

In the teaching on submission in marriage, there is a qualifying phrase - "Wives, submit yourselves unto your own husbands, as unto the Lord". This clearly handles the problem of the husband becoming a dictator, a tyrant, an oppressor. No woman is commanded to subject herself to that. Her subjection is "in the fear of God; (or in the Spirit of Christ;) .... as unto the Lord". Submission, on her part, pre-supposes the headship of love on his.

What then about the unmarried women? Who assumes the responsibility of headship and the covering this is designed to provide for them? Surely, that is the function of the Church? The unmarried women are covered by headship in the Body of Christ, as are all members of that Body. We all need headship. We all need covering.

Michael Griffiths, General Director of the Overseas Missionary Fellowship, has some helpful comments on this subject. He says - "In Ephesians, Paul is giving illustrations of various relationships within the Christian community - married couples, children and parents, servants and masters. These categories are not exhaustive and are not intended to exclude free men who have no masters, couples who may have no children or men without wives or women without

---

* Dealt with under separate cover. See footnote on page 156.

husbands - not just bachelors and spinsters, but also widowers and widows. Paul is merely giving three examples of some typical relationships involved within the community ....

"Even for unmarried first-generation Christians we are able to say that the congregation as the household of God provides for them a wonderful extended family in which they may feel wanted and at home, and have a satisfying role to play. All of us know any number of outstanding unmarried people who make a tremendous contribution to the growth and upbuilding of the congregational body through their sacrificial service. Not only are they themselves blessed by being members of the extended family of the household of God, but they also contribute much to the warm reality of the congregational fellowship. In this way everyone knows - young and old, married and single, widow and widower, child and orphan - that they belong wonderfully and delightfully to 'the household of God'. We need to remember that both marriage and being single are temporary states, for in heaven we neither marry nor are given in marriage (Matt.22:30), and that both states are described in 1 Corinthians 7:7 as a 'special gift' (the word is charisma)." *

SUBMISSION TO CHRIST'S HEADSHIP

"Therefore as the church is subject unto Christ, so let the wives be to their own husbands in every thing". Just as Christian marriage reflects the mystery of the vital relationship existing between Christ and His Church, so are those bound in the marriage tie called upon to take their example from the submissiveness of the Church to Christ.

If the Church goes forward in pride and its own carnal wisdom and is thus insubmissive to Christ her Lord, then all that is disorderly, unwholesome and fleshly emerge. If we are going to see Christian marriage established after God's order, married couples must witness in the fellowship of the Church, how beautifully and lovingly the Church is continuously subjecting herself to Christ her Lord.

* Michael Griffiths - "Cinderella With Amnesia", IVP 1977, pp.91,92.

When the Church is moving in the Spirit, and as the Body of Christ is subject in all things to the directive of Christ its Head, then there is a sweetness of grace upon all the members. This is manifest in all their relationships, resulting in a flow of divine blessing that speaks to all the married couples in that Body.

To such husbands and wives will come the desire to see fulfilled in their marriage, what is exemplified in the Church.

2   THE SACRIFICE OF LOVE   (5:25)

THE TRUE NATURE OF HEADSHIP

"Husbands, love your wives, even as Christ also loved the church". Here we have a clear insight into the true nature of headship in the marriage bond. It is definitely not one of authoritarianism, dictatorialism, domination or autocracy. It is a headship immersed in love - total, selfless, sacrificial, divine love.

The Church is subject to Christ because He loved it. He is its Saviour, protection, defence, safety, security, governing authority, victory; its very life and power. The Christian husband has the nature and life of Jesus in him. Because of this, he willingly and graciously applies himself to the role and responsibility of headship. This headship, immersed in love, is gracious, caring, protecting, sacrificing, covering.

THE EXAMPLE OF CHRIST'S HEADSHIP

"And gave himself for it". Here is the measure of the love of Christ. It is totally selfless and sacrificial. That portion can be translated 'and Himself gave up for her'. Such was His love, that He was prepared to abandon Himself, submit to the death of the Cross, pay the ransom price of her redemption, in order to purchase her for Himself.

There should be no problem of submission to Christ, because the members of the Body feel the warmth and the love of her Lord. "He is the Saviour of the body". When this is the true nature of headship in marriage,

166

there should never be any problem over wives submitting "to their own husbands in every thing".

3   THE GLORY OF LOVE   (5:26-30)

THE GLORY OF CHRIST REFLECTED IN HIS CHURCH

"That he might sanctify and cleanse it with the washing of water by the word, That he might present it to himself a glorious church, not having spot, or wrinkle, or any such thing; but that it should be holy and without blemish".

Here was the object of Christ's love. It was to come into this sin cursed, devil dominated, fallen world and redeem for Himself a people who would reflect the glory of that beautiful and perfect life of our Lord Jesus Christ. The whole purpose of the giving up of Himself was, that He might sanctify, or set apart for a divine purpose – the Church, and to cleanse it with the washing of water by the Word.

The love, that husbands are commanded to have for their wives, is as the love that Christ had for His Church when He gave Himself for it, for the express purpose of setting it apart for Himself, cleansing and presenting it to Himself "a glorious church, not having spot, or wrinkle, or any such thing". There should be a deep desire in the heart of every Christian husband to present his wife beautiful, pure and wholesome in every way. Such should be the relationship of love in marriage, that it will bring forth a glory and splendour otherwise unattainable.

We have already seen that such was the nature of the Father's covering in His Headship of Christ His Son, that Jesus submitted to that coming "not to do his own will, but the will of him that sent him". All His work and His words were wholly submitted to His Father. So, when Jesus spoke, He reflected and portrayed the words, works and will of His Father. Everything that He did, expressed His Father's heart. Everything about Jesus is the express image of His Father's Person.

It is in this spirit that wives are asked to submit to their husbands "as unto the Lord". This way, Jesus cleanses the Church by the washing of water, in or by the Word, i.e. the Word that He spoke and ministered. What a mighty ministry it was that Jesus brought in the Word which He spoke. By His Word the Church is cleansed and purified. By it the Church is set apart - a distinctive people for God's use. Everything about the work and words of Jesus conveyed the heart of His Father so much, that there was wrought, in love, something beautiful in those for whom He gave Himself, bringing them forth to be the people that would reveal His image - His glory.

THE GLORY OF THE HUSBAND REFLECTED IN HIS WIFE

"So ought men to love their wives as their own bodies. He that loveth his wife loveth himself. For no man ever yet hated his own flesh; but nourisheth and cherisheth it, even as the Lord the church".
It is wrong for men to demean or denigrate themselves. It is time for all men of God in the Church of Jesus Christ, to accept themselves for what God has made them in His grace. When they do that they will begin to have a new sense of honour and dignity about their role, their calling and their responsibility. Unless they are capable of self-respect, they will never be able to convey respect and love for their wives.

His wife, then, is his own flesh, "For no man ever yet hated his own flesh", says the Word, "but nourisheth and cherisheth it, even as the Lord the Church". Every Christian husband should give heed to this command of the Lord to love their wives. They are called to be nourishing and cherishing their wives. To the Corinthians the apostle Paul writes, that "a man is the image and glory of God: but the woman is the glory of the man". (1 Cor.11:7).

There is a tendency, in society to-day, for marriage to be treated carelessly and lightly. What a contrast is seen here in this glorious revelation of Christian marriage. When the marriage of couples, who are members in the Body of Christ, is in harmony with this Word of the Lord, it is most beautiful. Wives take on a new beauty, expressive of fulfilment and contentment. They are so at peace and blessed, that they are a joy to behold.

What is it that makes them so different, that they

reflect beauty, purity, security and stability in their character? Christ's giving up Himself for the Church was for the express purpose that He might present her to Himself "a glorious church". That word "glorious" means 'unsullied array' or 'inward glory'. The true Church of Jesus Christ never has to try to put a face on things. It will automatically reflect the inward glory and character of Christ, whose life and fulness indwells her.

So it is with wives in Christian marriage. If things are on God's terms, according to God's purpose, they will not have to struggle to convey an outward appearance, that does not truly reflect what is within. Everything about them will reflect the character and glory of that inward nature of love and grace, that makes Christian marriage what it is meant to be.

Does this not give the lie to the idea that the apostle Paul was a woman oppressor? There is no suggestion of inequality or partiality here. Husbands have their own distinctive role, just as wives have their distinctive role. One is not unequal to the other. They are just different. God has ordained it so. If the husband will fulfil his rightful function, and the wife her rightful role, rather than being suppressed, oppressed and dominated, she will be seen to be a woman fulfilled, satisfied, blessed and a revelation of the glory of true love in marriage.

4 THE BOND OF LOVE (5:31-33)

MARRIAGE - DIVINELY ORDAINED

"For this cause shall a man leave his father and mother, and shall be joined unto his wife, and they two shall be one flesh". Here we are taken right back to the beginning, where God made known His purpose for man. This quotation was taken from Genesis 2:24 and it is very apparent, that whatever problems modern man has with the Genesis account of creation, the apostle Paul had none of these. More than once does the apostle Paul refer back to this purpose of God in marriage.

Once man commits himself to his partner in life and having done so, from a basis of true manhood with all the maturity that that brings, together with a sense of responsibility that is called for in such an important decision, God ordained that such should leave father and mother and commit himself wholly to his wife. 'To cleave' means 'to cling to, or hold fast to'. The former domestic relationships give way to this new priority. Husband and wife now belong together in a distinctive, unique, intrinsic and united way. Literally, they become "one flesh" in the sight of God.

It is important to remember that Jesus Himself made reference to this same Scripture when answering the Pharisees in Matthew 19:3-6. He referred them right back to the beginning, to God's original intention, quoting this very Scripture, saying, "Wherefore they are no more twain, but one flesh. What therefore God hath joined together, let not man put asunder".

To-day when marriage is treated with such disrespect in some quarters and literally polluted and corrupted; or used by others as a convenience to further their own immoral ends, Christian couples would do well to give heed to the injunction of the Word of God and thus give adequate, due and responsible thought to it, before finally committing themselves to their life partner.

MARRIAGE - MYSTERY OF CHRIST AND HIS CHURCH

"This is a great mystery: but I speak concerning Christ and the church". Just as husband and wife are united together in an indissoluble bond, so is the Church bonded to Christ, "For we are members of His body, of his flesh, and of his bones". (Eph.5:30).

What a beautiful revelation is this. To what an elevated position is the apostle Paul guided to present the marriage of believers. Christian marriage is meant to reflect, in every aspect of its life, the nature of the union that binds Christ to His Church.

Those of us, who are known to be responsible ministers in the service of God, should remember that our ministry is not first seen in our preaching or our pastoral care for others. It is first seen, for those of us who are married, in how we live our married life.

170

We know that problems can arise continuously in Christian marriage, often due to either a dominating role by the husband, or an insubmissiveness on the part of the wife. Unless, however, this is understood and repented of, problems will continue and the marriage bond be adversely affected.

When husbands or wives have done their utmost to fulfil their rightful role, according to the grace of God available to them, and provided the applying of themselves to this in a responsible way is mutual, then there will be unfolded before the eyes of all, in a practical way, the Mystery of Christ and His Church.

Let the apostle Peter have the last word here. "Ye wives, be in subjection to your own husbands; that, if any obey not the word, they also may without the word be won by the conversation of the wives .... Likewise, ye husbands, dwell with them according to knowledge, giving honour unto the wife, as unto the weaker vessel, and as being **heirs together** of the grace of life; that your prayers be not hindered". (1 Peter 3:1-7).

Ephesians 6:1-9

1. Children, obey your parents in the Lord: for this is right.

2. Honour thy father and mother; which is the first commandment with promise;

3. That it may be well with thee, and thou mayest live long on the earth.

4. And, ye fathers, provoke not your children to wrath: but bring them up in the nurture and admonition of the Lord.

5. Servants, be obedient to them that are your masters according to the flesh, with fear and trembling, in singleness of your heart, as unto Christ;

6. Not with eyeservice, as menpleasers; but as the servants of Christ, doing the will of God from the heart;

7. With good will doing service, as to the Lord, and not to men:

8. Knowing that whatsoever good thing any man doeth, the same shall he receive of the Lord, whether he be bond or free.

9. And, ye masters, do the same things unto them, forbearing threatening: knowing that your Master also is in heaven; neither is there respect of persons with him.

CHAPTER 11

HOME AND BUSINESS

(Ephesians 6:1-9)

1. THE FAMILY   (6:1-4)

   Basic Relationship in the Family
   Childhood Respect in the Family
   Parental Responsibility in the Family

2. BUSINESS   (6:5-9)

   Basic Commitment in Business
   Servants' Loyalty in Business
   Masters' Impartiality in Business

CHAPTER 11

HOME AND BUSINESS

(Ephesians 6:1-9)

It is essential that we note the context of the portion with which we are now dealing. In chapter 9, we were dealing with the Spirit-filled life of the believers, and the outflow from that, which culminated in the text of chapter 5:21 "Submitting yourselves one to another in the fear of God".

One of the most important results, of living one's life in the fulness of the Holy Spirit, is that the believer is led into a right relationship with other believers. This was the case from the very first day of Pentecost, when the Holy Spirit was poured out upon the believers: "They continued stedfastly in ....fellowship ...." (Acts 2:42). So it is now. We have seen that, basic to proper relationships in the fellowship of the Body, is this matter of submission one to another. The moment people assert themselves, dominate and lord it over others, the unity, so essential to harmonious fellowship, is marred.

What is essential is that every one, in the fellowship of God's people, recognises the uniqueness and responsibility of the role of others in the fellowship. We should support each other and co-operate together in this and encourage one another, so that in each one's life there is a fulfilment of that to which God has called one. This, of course, happens only as we live our ongoing lives continuously in the fulness of the Holy Spirit, for it is as the grace and fruit of the Spirit are produced in us, that this is made possible.

Now what follows, from chapter 5:22 right on to chapter 6:9, is an unfolding of this principle of submission "one to another". We have already looked at that principle in Christian marriage. Here we are dealing with the very same subject in the family and in business. We must remember, however, that the apostle Paul is still talking to the Church. He is exhorting those who are Spirit-filled. He is counselling the believers, the members of the Body of Christ, concerning that which should be manifest in their behaviour in marriage, at home and in business.

1 THE FAMILY (6:1-4)

BASIC RELATIONSHIP IN THE FAMILY

It is interesting, therefore, to note that family life in the Christian sense should not be divorced from life in the Spirit. Parents should live their whole lives in the ongoing, infilling of the Spirit of God. The children too should grow up in this atmosphere. Why should we think it a thing incredible that children should be filled with the Holy Spirit, if they are being brought up in the nurture and admonition of the Lord? Surely, one should expect that the sense of godly fear pervading the atmosphere of the Christian home would influence and affect the children for good?

In these days of the latter day outpouring of the Spirit of God, multitudes of children are coming into the blessing of the Lord. Our children need this, if they are going to face in their adolescent life and early youth, the intrusion and invasion of subtle, evil and godless influences, pervading so much of society to-day. Children of this generation are having to face increasingly the 'abounding of iniquity' which was foretold by Jesus Himself. The prophetic insight that the apostle Paul had of the perilous times that would characterise the last days, is now being unfolded before our very eyes. (2 Tim.3:1-5). Let us not forget what our children are having to contend with in this generation.

CHILDHOOD RESPECT IN THE FAMILY

"Children, obey your parents in the Lord: for this is right". The word 'obey' is a command given in the present tense and means literally a 'coming under' what they hear said to them by their parents. In

175

other words, 'listen and do'. Therefore, 'obedience' accepts the discipline of heeding and carrying out instruction.

Here, too, we have to consider the problem of children being subject to parents who are wicked, neglectful and careless. Such people have no sense of family responsibility and are so much under the control of evil, that they cannot possibly behave as normal parents to their children. Local authorities have sometimes to take such children into care.

It is clear that this instruction is to children whose parents are "in the Lord". Such parents will manifest the conduct and the due responsibility characterised by the fruit of the Spirit, equally at home, as in the assembly. Indeed, such a home itself is an example of what the Church is meant to be like. In such a family, where there is a proper relationship between parents and children, the Church itself is manifestly shown to be a colony of heaven on earth. Right there in the home, God's Church is seen living and functioning in all the principles of grace, which are characteristic of fellowship in the Body of Christ.

"Honour thy father and mother; which is the first commandment with promise".

When Moses received the commandments from God for the children of Israel, the first three were concerned with the relationship of the people with Him. They were commanded not to have false gods, not to take the name of the Lord in vain, and to remember the sabbath day as being holy to the Lord. Then immediately following that, we have this commandment, "Honour thy father and thy mother: that thy days may be long upon the land which the Lord thy God giveth thee". (Exod.20:12).

It was God Himself who established marriage and the family. God established fatherly and motherly care for children, that would reflect the fatherly and motherly nature of Him, who made us to be His children and to be the objects of His love and delight. God wanted parents who would act with responsibility, honour, dignity, love and grace and whose children would appreciate and respect them in that, as they would grow up to the years of maturity.

To-day, there is a terrible breakdown in both marriage and home life and an increasing departure

from what God ordained and intended. The Christian
Church is called upon to express the true nature of
the fellowship that God has ordained at every level
of its life. Thus, His people can give expression to
this right at ground level, in family life, in the home.

We are reminded by the apostle Paul, that this
was the "first commandment with promise". The promise
was "That it may be well with thee, and thou mayest
live long on the earth". God Himself was concerned,
that children grow up to honour their father and
mother. For such, God promised special blessing, but
this is often marred in the kind of situations that
we face to-day. By the power of the Holy Spirit,
however, it is gloriously possible, and is most
beautiful to behold.

For many children growing into adolescence and
youth, they may look back on family life that has
not been like this. Often, it has been remarked upon,
that the problem of this generation is not just child
delinquency, but parental delinquency. In the midst
of all this, however, it is a delight when children
come to know the Lord. Even if they have not had
a Christian background, once the grace of God has
laid hold upon them, they begin to honour and respect
their parents as it was not possible for them to do
formerly.

PARENTAL RESPONSIBILITY IN THE FAMILY

"And, ye fathers, provoke not your children to
wrath: but bring them up in the nurture and
admonition of the Lord". Here is an appeal to
Christian parents to recognise the importance and
responsibility of their vocation in the home. How they
behave, before and toward their children, is
exceedingly important. Children need discipline, but
to speak of and exercise discipline over children, when
parents themselves are indisciplined, is to be utterly
irresponsible. We should all know that the best method
of instruction and guidance to others, is by example.
Even those, who are called to function with
responsibility in the Church, are called not to be
"lords over God's heritage", but to be "ensamples to
the flock". (1 Peter 5:3).

In the instruction to the fathers not to provoke

their children, the word 'provoke' is basically the same word as in chapter 4:26 - "Let not the sun go down upon your wrath", the word "wrath" meaning 'provocation to anger'.

Children need the Lord, because as we are clearly instructed in the Word, we are all born in sin and "shapen in iniquity". (Psalm 51:5;Romans 3:9). From the earliest days, children manifest evidences of a nature that is tainted by sin, hence the need for discipline and instruction. If they are being provoked by those who are responsible for their nurture, their welfare and their discipline, then that which is within them will develop and manifest itself in uncontrollable ways.

All believers need the wisdom of the Lord and the power of the Holy Spirit to enable them to be proper parents to their children. If they behave as parents who are "in the Lord" toward their children, in due course understanding comes, and as conviction by the Holy Spirit enters their young hearts and minds, they too will recognise their need of Jesus as Saviour and Lord and will confess that need and accept Him into their hearts and lives.

Thus the fathers are instructed to "bring them up", a word in the present tense meaning 'nourish' or 'educate'. They are to go on doing this responsibly, so that there will be no times of neglect in this area. This is a continuous responsibility while children are growing up. They are to be nourished in the 'training up', or the 'discipline', and admonition, or warning of the Lord.

Sadly, it is not like this in many homes. Thus, we have a society that the Word of God calls "crooked and perverse". Once, however, people come to recognise their need and submit to Christ as Lord, they become His disciples, His followers, His disciplined ones.

Both children and parents are thus commanded to reflect the true nature of Christ and His Church in home and family. May God give us all grace to fulfil this requirement. It can be and will be, as we go on to live our lives in the fulness of the Holy Spirit.

2 BUSINESS (6:5-9)

What kind of world was it that the apostle Paul came into and in which he was brought up? It is very clear that slavery abounded. Privileged people of affluence and note mostly employed the poorer classes as slaves. It was accepted by all as normal practice. In our Authorised Version they are referred to as "servants". This is another word for 'bondmen' or 'slaves'. A good example of this is Philemon's slave, who is called Onesimus. (Philemon 10,16).

It is quite remarkable that the apostle Paul just accepted as normal this political state of affairs. The apostle Paul sought to raise no political strife over it, nor did he commend civil disobedience in respect of it, however right or wrong that might have been. He gives us his standing in this respect clearly in 1 Corinthians 7:21-24.

BASIC COMMITMENT IN BUSINESS

The apostle Paul's clear instruction here, to slaves and to masters alike, was that slaves should behave as Christian slaves; and masters as Christian masters. As slaves, their service should be "as unto Christ", and as masters, they should behave with the same grace as their Master .... in heaven.

In our modern society, slavery as such is largely abolished, but the principle of servants and masters remains. Business could not be effected in an efficient and co-ordinated way without responsible personnel, who have authority for direction, instruction and for the conduct of all business affairs. Employees are literally servants in the business. If there is not due recognition of each one's rightful role, either of responsible management, or faithful and loyal service, then possibly there will be conflict and anarchy prevailing.

In all secular business, masters and servants are called upon to act and conduct their affairs, manifesting forth the grace of our Lord Jesus Christ. The true principles of submission and authority operate here as much as anywhere else. The Church should be a living example of all that is characteristic of submission and authority, as its members relate

179

aright to the Lord and to one another.

SERVANTS' LOYALTY IN BUSINESS

"Servants, be obedient to them that are your masters according to the flesh, with fear and trembling, in singleness of your heart, as unto Christ". This word 'obey' is the same as that word in the injunction to the children called upon to obey their parents. It implies a readiness to accept the authority of their masters and to listen and do according to their wishes, with due respect for them and in simplicity of heart *"as unto Christ".*

In society to-day, it is very sad to see the chaos continuously created by both covetousness and greed, sometimes in those who own and manage business, and sometimes in those employed: that which is manifested as rebellion and disruption, created by those who do not know Christ and who could not serve, in this kind of simplicity of heart, as to Him.

Those who are truly living their life in the fulness of the Spirit, will understand what follows here, for their spirit will witness with this perfectly. The apostle Paul says, *"not with eye service"* and that word literally means 'service rendered only while under inspection'. This suggests that there are those who will only render faithful and loyal service provided they are watched, and that all that is done is seen by those to whom they are in subjection. The word for *"menpleasers"* means 'seeking favour with men'. This is not how Christian workers are called upon to serve.

The apostle Paul himself called his own commitment to Christ as that of a slave to his master. He referred to himself as a prisoner of Jesus Christ (4:1), just as he outlines in 1 Corinthians that those who are slaves should remember that they are, first of all, Christ's servants. (1 Cor.7:22). Thus they are called upon to work for their earthly masters as *"servants of Christ"*, representing Him, aware that they are not serving men, but serving their Lord. They are seeking, not favour with men, but living at all times pleasing to Him, who is their Lord and Master.

"Doing the will of God from the heart". This word *"doing"* is in the present tense and means

'continuously doing their service on the basis of commitment to Christ', i.e. doing the will of God from the heart. Every part of one's soul life: desires, emotions, affections - everything must be involved in one's service, even if it be a secular job. Believers should be seen to serve with joy and with trust, faithfulness and loyalty.

The Lord is no man's debtor. We cannot outgive God. If our service in business, whether we be bond or free, servant or master, is rendered "as to the Lord" from the heart, there is no doubt but that what he gives, he shall receive from the Lord.

The Spirit of Christ is the spirit of giving. "The Son of Man came not to be ministered unto, but to minister, and to give His life a ransom for many". But what did He gain for Himself, in the giving of Himself, in that kind of service and ministry? He loved the Church and gave Himself for it, "that he might present it to himself a glorious church". What Satan destroyed in God's creational glory in man, Christ by redemption has restored to God again. "Unto our God and Father will be glory in the church by Christ Jesus". This is the true spirit, in which service should be rendered in the world by Christian masters and servants.

MASTERS' IMPARTIALITY IN BUSINESS

"And, ye masters, do the same thing unto them, forbearing threatening: knowing that your Master also is in heaven; neither is there respect of persons with him". Christian masters, managers, proprietors and owners are called upon to fulfil their responsible function in the way in which Jesus did. They are to give up, or dispense with, threats or harshness of language.

This word "knowing" is mentioned in this passage twice - "knowing that whatsoever good ....", and "knowing that your Master also is in heaven". This means that they are not to conduct business in ignorance of the Lord. They will be aware of what God has promised to those who faithfully serve Him and who conduct their lives in the light of His presence, submitting to His example. They know that, with their Master who is in heaven, there is no *partiality, no respect of persons. Everyone under their charge is treated with equal respect, love and care.*

When, as either workers or employers, we render service to each other "as to the Lord", then we are, in commerce and industry, a practical example for all to see, of what the Church of Christ on earth is like. The Church is not an exclusive institution, unable to relate in a world where Satan rules in many hearts and lives. It is God's Church, ruling in the midst of the enemies of the Lord, in righteousness, in purity, in honour and in grace.

10. Finally, my brethren, be strong in the Lord, and in the power of his might.

11. Put on the whole armour of God, that ye may be able to stand against the wiles of the devil.

12. For we wrestle not against flesh and blood, but against principalities, against powers, against the rulers of the darkness of this world, against spiritual wickedness in high places.

13. Wherefore take unto you the whole armour of God, that ye may be able to withstand in the evil day, and having done all, to stand.

14. Stand therefore, having your loins girt about with truth, and having on the breastplate of righteousness;

15. And your feet shod with the preparation of the gospel of peace;

16. Above all, taking the shield of faith, wherewith ye shall be able to quench all the fiery darts of the wicked.

17. And take the helmet of salvation, and the sword of the Spirit, which is the word of God;

18. Praying always with all prayer and supplication in the Spirit, and watching thereunto with all perseverance and supplication for all saints;

19. And for me, that utterance may be given unto me, that I may open my mouth boldly, to make known the mystery of the gospel,

20. For which I am an ambassador in bonds: that therein I may speak boldly, as I ought to speak.

21. But that ye also may know my affairs, and how I do, Tychicus, a beloved brother and faithful minister in the Lord, shall make known to you all things:

22. Whom I have sent unto you for the same purpose, that ye might know our affairs, and that he might comfort your hearts.

23. Peace be to the brethren, and love with faith, from God the Father and the Lord Jesus Christ.

24. Grace be with all them that love our Lord Jesus Christ in sincerity. Amen

CHAPTER 12

CONFLICT AND TRIUMPH

(Ephesians 6:10,11)

1. DIVINE PROVISION FOR THE CONFLICT   (6:10,11)

        Internal Provision
        External Provision

2. SPIRITUAL NATURE OF THE CONFLICT   (6:12)

        Not with flesh and blood
        But with forces of darkness
        In the heavenlies

3. ASSURANCE OF VICTORY IN THE CONFLICT   (6:13)

4. ARMOUR PROVIDED FOR THE CONFLICT   (6:14-17)

        Truth for the Loins
        Righteousness as a Breastplate
        Gospel of Peace for the Feet
        Faith as a Shield
        Salvation as a Helmet
        Word of God as a Sword

5. PRAYER COVER FOR THE CONFLICT   (6:18-20)

6. MUTUAL COMFORT IN THE CONFLICT   (6:21-24)

CHAPTER 12

CONFLICT AND TRIUMPH

(Ephesians 6:10-24)

Before we consider the various aspects of teaching concerning 'spiritual conflict', let us briefly examine the context that leads up to this introductory word - "finally", for this word means 'for, or of the rest'. In other words, there is something more to say. The apostle Paul has been leading up to this and he is about to disclose it. It is a matter of great importance and we must take special note.

The context, of this subject of 'spiritual conflict', stems from the ministry on the Holy Spirit, at which we have already looked in chapter 9. We saw there that the natural outflow of the ongoing life in the Spirit for all the members of the Body of Christ issues in open worship, continuous thanksgiving and mutual submission.

In chapter 10 we looked at the meaning of submission and oneness in the marriage bond. In chapter 11 we looked at the meaning of submission and co-operation in the family. We have seen, therefore, that the principles and practice of submission and authority are absolutely vital to true spiritual fellowship in the Body of Christ. This being clearly understood, we are brought to this very important and illuminating subject of 'spiritual conflict'.

It is not without significance, that at least two other scriptures, dealing with this same subject of spiritual conflict have, in their context, the emphasis of submission to God and to one another.

In the teaching of James chapters 2, 3 and 4, quite considerable stress is made on how believers should relate one to the other; and of particular concern is their attitude to one another. In chapter 4, James begins - "From whence come wars and fightings among you? Then he says "God resisteth the proud, but giveth grace unto the humble. Submit yourselves therefore to God. Resist the devil, and he will flee from you". (James 4:6,7). We cannot properly submit "one to another" unless we are in submission to God. Only in submission to Him are we recipients of the grace that enables us to harmonise together and thus mutually to respect one another. Fellowship together is about sharing, caring and trusting one another. In fact, true fellowship means that we commit our lives to one another, as well as to the Lord, even to the point of being willing to "lay down our life" for one another. When fellowship has that kind of binding together of love, then there is little problem about resisting the devil. In that atmosphere, there are no fleshly or carnal gaps in our relationships that the evil one can exploit and use to wreak havoc.

The other important teaching, in this connection, is by the apostle Peter who instructs, "Be sober, be vigilant; because your adversary the devil, as a roaring lion, walketh about, seeking whom he may devour: Whom resist stedfast in the faith". (1 Peter 5:8,9). Again, all the context here is about the nature of fellowship in the assembly of God's people.

The elders are instructed to behave in the spirit of their master, the Good Shepherd, thus being "ensamples to the flock" and doing faithfully the work of shepherding. The younger are exhorted to submit themselves "unto the elder" and all are instructed "Be subject one to another, and be clothed with humility: for God resisteth the proud, and giveth grace to the humble". (1 Peter 5:5).

This is the background to the teaching on resisting the devil, for in rightness of fellowship with God and with one another, we are under the covering of the Headship of Christ in His body. There, we are safe. Outside of that, we become easy prey for the evil one.

1   DIVINE PROVISION FOR THE CONFLICT   (6:10,11)

INTERNAL PROVISION

"Be strong in the Lord, and in the power of his

might". The verb means 'be empowered'. It is a command in the present tense, like that in chapter 5:18, and means 'be continuously being empowered'. The command in the middle voice suggests that we ourselves must also be possessed with the power which is God's. We have to be empowered in the Lord, and in the strength of His might, for in ourselves we are not sufficient for the conflict. We would never survive it in our own strength. Only by this empowering will the Body of Christ on earth cope with the challenge.

EXTERNAL PROVISION

"Put on the whole armour of God, that ye may be able to stand against the wiles of the devil". Here the word meaning 'clothe yourselves', as in Ephesians 4:24, is spoken to the whole Body. It is in the plural form, is commanded and is something to which all believers are called upon to respond. This is an action meant to be done once and for all. In other words, never be found with the armour off. Clothe yourselves with it once and for all.

"Put on the whole armour of God". From the word 'armour' - panoplian, our English word 'panoply' is derived and simply means 'complete armour'. We should never be found with our armour incomplete, for there is armour provided for every emergency and contingency in this spiritual conflict that we face as the Body of Christ.

This panoply is to enable the saints to "stand against the wiles of the devil". The word 'wiles' - methodias, is almost like our English word method and means 'stratagems', or 'artifices' of the devil. Everything about Satan's work is deceitful, and this always is the hallmark of all his activity. (Rev.12:9). The nature of this conflict is such, that believers can neither stand in their own strength, nor cope with the artifices of the enemy, without "the whole armour of God".

This is what we saw in chapter 4:22–24. The putting off of the former manner of life, the "old man", that carnal nature which operates through soul and body in our conduct, behaviour and relationships amongst people, was followed by the instruction in verse 23 "Be renewed in the spirit of your mind". Then, putting on the "new man" means that our continuing conduct and relationships are all that is righteous and holy. This is because we allowed the inner shrine of our spirit to be indwelt and renewed by the Holy Spirit. We need strength and renewal constantly. Only then can we cope with facing up to the challenge of a world benighted and in darkness.

Thus, we need to be "strengthened with his might .... in the inner man", so that our spiritual life is strong in the Lord. Then the Church, on the offensive against the enemy and covered by the panoply of God, has full provision for every contingency. This is vital, for there are many unexpected, unusual and almost inconceivable stratagems devised by the enemy in his attempts to resist and repel the ongoing Church, as it moves forward in the power of the Holy Ghost.

We must "put on the whole armour", so that in all our relationships with one another, in all the areas where we touch each other and communicate together, we can, without weakness or fear, face up to this evil age. As a provision for all our thinking, attitudes, motives and behaviour, we should be well armed - in order to cope with the stratagems of evil.

2 SPIRITUAL NATURE OF THE CONFLICT (6:12)

NOT WITH FLESH AND BLOOD

"For we wrestle not against flesh and blood". How utterly important it is for every member of the Body of Christ to take note of this. The wrestling, the struggle, the contest is not to us one of "flesh and blood", although without the Spirit of God and without the "armour of God", we may well imagine it to be so. This is part of the strategy of Satan, who is waiting for the unwitting and unprepared in order to exploit them.

Many people have naively thought that life in the fulness of the Holy Spirit is, for them, the end of all their problems. Undoubtedly, in the fulness of the Spirit there is life, there is power, there is blessing, there is joy, there is a new awareness of God, a new sense of closeness and relationship to Him. There is, indeed, grace to enable us to communicate one with the other and to fellowship in righteousness and holiness, in peace and in blessing. Yes, this is true and all this is so very wonderful and exciting to the believer who comes into this experience for the first time, but it is so easy to imagine that, now being so well equipped and provided for, there will be no more serious trouble with which it will be necessary to cope.

Nothing could be further from the truth. In fact, to have lived a nominal Christian life, even to have been a regular church attender, may never have allowed for the possibility of seeing the true nature of what spiritual life is about, or of the real enemy of Christ's Church, who is out to thwart the purpose of God and endeavour thus to destroy His people. It is utterly essential that those who are entering into a charismatic experience for the first time, be prepared for the depth of conflict to which they may now have been introduced. While they should never fear it, nor be alarmed at the understanding they now have, nor be amazed that certain people react to them now differently than they had formerly done, at the same time it is exceedingly important that they understand what is happening out there in the real world, for ignorance is not really bliss.

Never forget that the real conflict is not with flesh and blood. It is not basically with people themselves. We must be prepared to see behind what is happening to and through people. So much of what has gone on in so-called church life has been nothing but contention, bitterness and strife, just as the apostle Paul describes it in Galatians 5. Such Galatian-type bondages, that the Church has been subject to, have sometimes created carnality and fleshly attitudes and behaviour in the fellowship of God's people. Warfare, then, descends to a flesh and blood level and in that sense there is constant tension and division. That is why the apostle James says that the wisdom that is not from above is "earthly, sensual, devilish", and is characterised by "envying, strife, confusion and every evil work". (James 3).

BUT WITH FORCES OF DARKNESS

"Against principalities, against powers, against the rulers of the darkness of this world, against spiritual wickedness in high places". Here we see clearly the true enemy. Rulers, authorities, powers that hold sway in the darkness of this world. It is against spiritual wickedness "in the heavenlies".

In chapter 2 of the epistle, we saw clearly that what is ruling in the hearts of the people of disobedience, obstinacy and rebellion towards God, is the spirit of "the prince of the power of the air". This, in a fuller way, is what is comprehended here in our text. It is the spirit of anti-God and anti-Christ.

IN THE HEAVENLIES

How can the members of the Body cope with these evil powers when they are clearly described as operating "in the heavenlies"? This phrase, in the original text, is exactly as we have seen in four other places previously in this epistle. Here we refer back to our summary in chapter 1.

1. "Blessed with all spiritual blessings in the heavenlies in Christ". (1:3). Clearly, this is the Church's sphere of life.

2. "He set him at his own right hand in the heavenlies". (1:20). Here we see that the reason for the Church's sphere of life being "in the heavenlies", is that this is where Christ Himself is in His risen, ascended glory, power and authority.

3. "He made us sit together in the heavenlies in Christ Jesus". (2:6). Thus, "in Christ", this is the Church's true position. This is what makes the Body of Christ a colony of heaven on earth.

4. "Now unto the principalities and powers in the heavenlies might be known by the church the manifold wisdom of God". (3:10). Clearly, the Church that is being built by Christ Himself, here and now, displays to all principalities and powers in the heavenlies, "the manifold wisdom of God". The forces of darkness, therefore, will not like this and seek by every stratagem still to destroy what is now indestructible.

5. "For we wrestle .... against spiritual wickedness in the heavenlies". (6:12). It was essential that the

apostle Paul wait until this point in his epistle, to bring such an unfolding of the nature of this spiritual conflict and the sphere in which it is waged. To start looking at chapter 6, without understanding the meaning of life "in the heavenlies" from the previous texts, could be quite devastating. Once we understand, however, that we belong "in Christ", we belong "in the heavenlies", we are reigning now "in Christ in the heavenlies": by the time we come into chapter 6, we have nothing to fear.

There we see that all authority is in Christ's hands whose fulness indwells His Church. His ruling authority and power is in His people. Physically and mentally we dwell on earth. Spiritually we reside "in the heavenlies". And just as all powers and authorities are under Christ's feet, so in Christ are they under ours, His Church.

That is why in chapter 1:22,23 it is said "He .... is head over all things to the church, Which is his body, the fulness of him that filleth all in all". That authority, that Headship, that power is vested in the Church, the Body of Christ. Thus in chapter 6, the believers come into the place of awareness of the overcoming power, that belongs to them in Christ the Lord by the power of the Holy Spirit.

3   ASSURANCE OF VICTORY IN THE CONFLICT   (6:13)

Wherefore take unto you the whole armour of God, that ye may be able to withstand in the evil day, and having done all, to stand". Once again the word 'wherefore' means 'because of this'. In the light of the revelation now unfolded, of the true nature of this conflict and the sphere in which it is waged, the believers are exhorted and appealed to. In fact, more than exhorted. The word is in the imperative mood and in the aorist tense and means 'take up the whole armour of God and do not under any circumstances put it off'. "That ye may be able to withstand". The word for 'withstand' means - 'to stand against' the enemy in the day of evil.

"And having done all, to stand". "Having done all" means 'having worked out' or 'having subdued or conquered', then - "to stand". There is no *suggestion here of being overcome by the enemy, or of being weak in the conflict. All the teaching here is about the strength of the Spirit of God and the completeness of the panoply of God, which enables every member of the Body to stand in the kind of way that will overcome every device, stratagem, attack or opposition of the evil one, and still be standing.*

4 ARMOUR PROVIDED FOR THE CONFLICT (6:14-17)

TRUTH FOR THE LOINS

"Stand therefore, having your loins girt about with truth". Where believers are concerned, there can be no admittance of falsehood or deception, because this would give immediate ground to the evil one. All such questionable things have to be immediately detected, exposed, confessed, repented of and renounced.

Unless our loins are girded about by truth our spiritual lives will become very vulnerable. The inner life and shrine of the spirit, as it relates to the Spirit of God, must be guarded at all costs. There must be no compromise here.

RIGHTEOUSNESS AS A BREASTPLATE

"And having on the breastplate of righteousness". Here, where all our emotional and soul life, our desires and affections are seated; where all the issues of life proceed from; by which we conduct our vital relationships with others and from which our conduct in this world springs forth: we must be covered completely by His righteousness. Christ Himself has become our righteousness, our complete covering of righteousness. (Rom.10:4;1 Cor.1:30).

Let us ever remember that the sceptre of righteousness is the sceptre of His kingdom. All the ways of the Lord are right and true altogether. While we stand in His righteousness, in this area we are safe from every exploitation of the enemy. We can live a social and moral life before God and men - one that upholds the sceptre of His righteousness.

GOSPEL OF PEACE FOR THE FEET

"And your feet shod with the preparation of the gospel of peace". The word for "shod" conveys the idea of binding on something under the soles of our feet. This indicates that the conflict, in which the believer is engaged, does not in the slightest degree hinder his activity, his movements, his commission to go into all the world and preach the gospel, the good news.

In Romans 10:15 the apostle Paul takes up the strain of Isaiah 52 - "How beautiful are the feet of them that preach the gospel of peace, and bring glad tidings of good things". The Church is called upon to be well shod, fully prepared with the gospel of peace to men. That was the message of the angels when Jesus was born in Bethlehem of Judaea. "Peace, good will toward men".

The Church is not at war with the people. This has been clearly pointed out already. We are not wrestling against "flesh and blood". The warfare is a spiritual one and is against the powers of darkness. These powers dominate and captivate to destroy our fellow men and women. The Church has a responsibility to carry a gospel of peace, good news, good tidings from God to mankind.

There can be no preparation of the gospel of peace without first knowing and experiencing that peace for ourselves. That is all part of the preparation. The true believer has this already settled.

He has already accepted and appropriated to himself the peace provided by Him who is the Prince of Peace.

FAITH AS A SHIELD

"Above all, taking the shield of faith, wherewith ye shall be able to quench all the fiery darts of the wicked". The word for 'taking' is in the aorist tense and means - 'having taken up'. The concept is, that the shield of faith has already been taken up for overall protection.

This is the only protection against doubt, unbelief, deception, fear and all the things that promote distress, tension and strife. Without this shield of faith, there are areas in the believers' lives that could become vulnerable. Having taken up this shield and using it to protect themselves, believers will find that, however fiery these missiles that are sent by the wicked one, all will be destroyed. Believers should never be alarmed that such burning missiles are hurled at them, but they should ever remember the source from which they come and never refrain from using the shield for full and complete protection.

SALVATION AS A HELMET

"And take the helmet of salvation". The preposition 'peri' that is attached to this word in the Greek text indicates that this helmet covers the whole of the head. In chapter 3 we looked thoroughly into the nature of the salvation and the greatness of this salvation for the believers here and now. The enemy's strategy is to oppress us in subtle ways, thus to confuse our thinking processes and unsettle our minds.

When we consider the wonder of God's salvation for His people, for His Church, we will refuse to accept the insinuations, deceptions and accusations of the evil one. We will say, as in Revelation, "Now is come salvation, and strength, and the kingdom of our God, and the power of his Christ". (Rev.12:10). We will recognise afresh the total adequacy of the blood of Christ to have forgiven and cleansed us completely and to go on keeping us clean as we walk in the light.

When our head is covered with the helmet of salvation, we will realise that, though we were "dead in trespasses and sins", we have now been made alive with Christ. We have been raised with Him. We are seated now "in the heavenlies". This is what our salvation is about. It is God's provision for all who have been subject to the evil one's destructive design, but we can be assured, at all times, of the completeness of our salvation, deliverance and healing.

WORD OF GOD AS A SWORD

"And the sword of the Spirit, which is the word of God". In the armour of God there is the provision of the sword. The Word of God is called the "sword of the spirit", because it is the Holy Spirit who makes it what it is really meant to be. Without the Spirit, the Word of God can be itself a letter that kills in the believer's life. But in the power of the Spirit, life is imparted to the believer and it becomes a weapon with which to destroy the enemy.

This is how Jesus dealt with the tempter in the wilderness, as recorded by the gospel writers. He said, "It is written". The Holy Spirit inspired a particular word from the Scriptures that had to be spoken out. This is the 'rhēma' Word of God spoken of here. The words that Jesus quoted were there all the time in Deuteronomy, but it was His quoting of them, His use of them at the right time and place, that defeated the enemy.

So it is with the believers in the Church. What God has said, or what God is saying must be spoken out. That is why Jesus gave us the instruction, as recorded by Mark, about speaking to the mountain and commanding it, by word of mouth, to be removed. To such He promised, that those who do not doubt in their heart, should have exactly what they say. This is a word that springs forth from the faith of God imparted to them. (Mark 11:23).

All kinds of mountains, all kinds of opposition, all kinds of suggestions and insinuations appear before one or come at one, but by the Word of God spoken out, confessed, commanding, the enemy is put to flight before our very eyes.

5   PRAYER COVER FOR THE CONFLICT   (6:18–20)

Anyone that does not faithfully engage in prayer, in the way the apostle Paul enjoins, has not really any insight into the spiritual nature of the conflict in which the Church is engaged. There is an emphasis here on prayer and supplication. In fact, a literal rendering of verse 18 would be 'By all prayer and supplication praying'. The verb is in the continuous present tense and means 'a continuing prayer life'. This is added to by the words 'in every season in the spirit, and unto this watching with all perseverance and supplication for all saints'.

The whole Body is involved in prayer. Every member is involved in the prayer life. And the concern is "for all saints". The praying is in all seasons and applied, in a continuous tense, by all believers. This prayer life is also "in the Spirit". It is that natural outflow of the inward work of the Holy Spirit, by whom we are continuously being "filled".

'In the Spirit' or 'with the Spirit' simply means that we are one together with the Spirit of God, in all that He is doing in connection with the whole Body of Christ. It brings us to a mutual concern for one another before the Lord. It brings us to a place of supplication.

The word supplication is used twice in this text. It means that, being constantly conscious of our need and of being humbled before God, there comes a cry from our hearts for the need of the whole Church, the whole Body. Our awareness of the need for the Body should not make us critical or condemnatory in our attitudes one to another, but it should bring us to our knees in vital prayer and supplication "with all perseverance" for each other and for the whole Church.

Then the apostle says, "and for me" - huper emou. The preposition 'huper' used with this genitive pronoun means 'over me' and literally is a call from the apostle Paul to be covered with prayer. Why did he need the prayer of the saints? 'That to me may be given a word, or an utterance, in the act of opening my mouth with boldness, to make known in a decisive kind of way the mystery of the gospel'. People are blinded by the god of this world. They could not see, or understand, that the apostle Paul had a commission from God to give an unfolding ministry, thus to enlighten the eyes of many who were blind and in darkness.

"For", or 'over this', "I am an ambassador in bonds". This means, 'I perform ambassadorial duties in a chain'. Although bound by this chain, he believed that prayer would enable him to be bold, to speak the Word of the Lord and the gospel in an unfettered way. The apostle Paul wanted nothing to hinder the fulfilment of that for which he had been commissioned by God.

6   MUTUAL COMFORT IN THE CONFLICT   (6:21-24)

These final verses of the epistle are most touching. There is no doubt about the nature of the conflict, nor about the assurance of victory, nor about the empowering of the Holy Spirit, that enables the members of the Body of Christ to stand overcomingly in the evil day. They are, however, very human people who have to live out their lives and fulfil their holy calling in this real world system dominated by sin and the powers of darkness.

Just like Jesus after the devil tempted Him in the wilderness, "Angels came and ministered unto Him", (Matt.4:11), so with all the saints and servants of God: they need the comfort, understanding and strength afforded them by other members of the Body.

On one occasion, previous to this, while in the process of pursuing his apostolic calling, the apostle Paul declared that he longed to see the saints in Rome, not only that he might minister to them, but that he might be comforted by the mutual faith of both them and himself. (Rom.1:8-12). He desired both to comfort and to be comforted.

Here in our text, the apostle Paul had already expressed concern - "Wherefore I desire that ye faint not at my tribulations for you, which is your glory". (Eph.3:13). He had such a care for the churches, that he did not want discouragement to come to them through the adverse things that were happening to him.

Thus, (again in our text) he expresses such concern that they be fully informed concerning his affairs and how and what he is doing, that he sent Tychicus to them for this very thing, or this "same purpose".

Tychicus was one of the party who travelled with the apostle Paul in his missionary journey in Asia. (Acts 20:4). Here was a brother available to the apostle, to be sent out in ministry charges to other ministering brethren such as Titus. (Titus 3:12). Also, in the apostle's letter to Timothy from the prison, he declares: "And Tychicus have I sent to Ephesus". (2 Tim.4:12).

So he is referred to as "a beloved brother and faithful minister in the Lord". What an important role such faithful, responsible brethren fulfil in the Body of Christ.

Such a man too was Timothy, for the apostle said: "I have no man like-minded, who will naturally care for your state". (Phil.2:19-23).

Epaphroditus was another of like calibre, "For he longed after you all, and was full of heaviness .... Because for the work of Christ he was nigh unto death ...." (Phil.2:25-30).

Tychicus' ministry amongst them would not only enlighten them and give them fuel for prayer, but would literally comfort - i.e. encourage and strengthen them in the faith, and give them heart-comfort.

In the final, closing words of the epistle, the apostle comes full circle from his salutation at the beginning and expresses himself in the same words of peace, love, faith and grace.

"Peace be to the brethren, and love with faith, from God the Father and the Lord Jesus Christ. Grace (be) with all them that love (and keep on loving) our Lord Jesus Christ in sincerity - i.e. constantly, unfailingly. AMEN".

THE VISION GLORIOUS

(Ephesians 3:1-13)

The vision glorious of the Church,
It captivates our inmost heart;
Such riches we can never search,
But, wondrous Grace, we share a part.

The myst'ry now no more concealed,
Apostles, prophets hath made known,
What God's own Spirit hath revealed,
Eternal wonders He hath shewn.

One fellowship, indwelt by God,
Not strangers now, but 'UNITY',
Divinely blended through the blood,
Christ is our Head, His Body we.

Now to the powers of heavenly height,
The Church displays God's majesty;
Divinest wisdom, Infinite,
Revealed by saints through Grace so free.

O how we yearn that all men see -
This fellowship beyond our ken,
In this - to Him, the Glory be,
Through Christ, eternally, Amen!

Written by the author during the early part of his ministry in Peterhead, Aberdeenshire, January 1957-August 1959. A hymn tune was composed by him at the same time which he called 'PETERHEAD'. Copies of this are available on application.